LONDON'S RAILWAYS

Then and Now

Also by Edwin Course

Railways Then & Now (Batsford, 1979)
The Railways of Southern England Vol. I, II and III (Batsford, 1973, 1974, 1976)
London Railways (Batsford, 1962)

Edwin Course

LONDON'S RAILWAYS

Then and Now

B.T. BATSFORD LTD, LONDON

To my son, Martin Charles Andrew,
who studies and supports our railways

ISBN 0 7134 5257 9

Typeset by Tek-Art Ltd, Kent
and printed in Great Britain by
Anchor Brendon Ltd
Tiptree, Essex
for the publishers
B.T. Batsford Ltd.
4 Fitzhardinge Street
London W1H 0AH

CONTENTS

CONTENTS

Chapter five
South West London and beyond

ACKNOWLEDGEMENTS

I am particularly grateful to my friend Alan A. Jackson, for his help and advice in writing this book and also for examining the text. With regard to dates I am greatly indebted to Mr H.V. Borley, whose knowledge of the chronology of London railways is unequalled. For both typing and assistance in reaching so many parts of the London railway system, and also for support and encouragement, I am most grateful to Pam Moore.

The photographs are credited to the following – 107 (A.W. Burgess); 19, 25, 29, 100 (Henry Casserley); 65, 68 (F. Church); 44 (J.V. Horn); 35, 112 (Rev. J.V. Hall), 2, 4, 5, 10, 11, 16, 17, 23, 24, 31, 33, 36, 38, 41, 43, 47, 48, 50, 55, 59, 60, 63, 66, 70, 71, 75, 88, 91, 98, 101, 111, 115 (Alan A. Jackson); 42, 82, 99, 102, 104, 110, 114 (Alan A. Jackson collection); 106 (J.H. Price); 15, 21, 79, 84, 87, 94 (H.J. Patterson-Rutherford). Of the remainder, some are from my collection, and the rest were taken for this book.

Collecting the material was an interesting experience, with visits to many parts of the London railway system. I particularly thank Mr Bolton of the BR Property Board for access to St Pancras Chambers, and also the numerous railwaymen met on various railway premises. I am sorry that lack of space has made it impossible to include all the sites visited but hope that those selected will serve to portray the changing scene on London's Railways.

E.C.

INTRODUCTION

The camera catches a moment in time; it records what was to be seen at a particular place at one point in its history. During the time, perhaps less than one hundredth of a second, for which the shutter of the camera remains open, the degree of change, such as the movement of a train, may be ignored. This book consists of a collection of such views of railways, in and around London, taken between 1905 and 1986. The selection has been chosen for the way in which the various views record the changing railway scene. A balance has been sought between station interiors and exteriors, track and signals, trains and all the other components of the railway scene, including a railway hotel. The old pre-grouping companies ceased to exist at the end of 1922, but their policies and distinctive characters have left their mark, and because of this, sites on all the pre-grouping companies that served London have been included.

Perhaps an even more fundamental distinction may be based on the different parts of London. For the purpose of this book, London has been divided into a central area and four sectors — north west and north east; south west and south east. The River Thames provides an effective boundary, although many of the southern companies had stations on the north side of the river. Perhaps the most obvious contrast between north and south is the concentration of underground railways north of the river, and in particular, in the north west sector. This was partly due to physical factors: the clay soil of the north lent itself more readily to tunnelling than the wet gravels which frequently occur south of the river. Company policies were also significant, in particular the aloof attitude to seeking mass suburban traffic displayed by the Great Western and the London and North Western Railways for so many years.

Between the wars, most railway development was executed by the Southern Railway, created by the grouping at the beginning of 1923, and by the railways of the Underground Group (included in London Transport from 1933). The Southern mainly, and the Underground Group entirely, gained their revenue from passenger traffic, which suffered less than freight during the years of trade depression. Furthermore, the Southern and the Underground Group were operating in the more prosperous parts of the country — a world of expanding light industry and office work — compared with the traditional industrial areas of the north. Even within the London area, there were contrasts. For instance, when the LNE was closing a long established service in the dockland area, new underground lines were being planned to penetrate LNE territory in North London.

Although the first tube railway had been built south of the Thames, it was the Southern Railway that made the most determined effort to keep the Underground Group at bay. The policy of collaboration followed by the GW and the LNW before and during the First World War perhaps reflected their traditional lack of enthusiasm for local traffic on their main lines. Between the wars, first the newly formed LMS and later the LNE agreed to the transfer of traffic to underground trains.

While the concentration of underground railways provides the most striking contrast between the north and south of 'railway' London, other differences are noticeable. For instance, from the opening of the London and Greenwich Railway in 1836, it was usual for the southern companies to reach their terminals by constructing viaducts over the crowded streets of the inner area. In contrast, north of the river, such stations as Kings Cross, Euston and St. Pancras were reached through tunnels. To the east, the original terminus at Bishopsgate was joined to a viaduct, but the later extension to Liverpool Street used a tunnel. Another distinction was provided by the ways in which the northern and southern companies pursued the policy of maintaining terminals in both the City and the West End of London. The southern companies, because of the vital importance of London suburban traffic to their revenues, built their own lines to the City and West End. The LSW, however, with its higher class and longer distance suburban traffic differed from the other three southern companies. It finally reached the City by means of an associated tube railway, the Waterloo and City, which was not opened until 1898. The GW, Midland and GN all extended their trains over the underground Metropolitan Railway to reach the City. The LNW used a surface railway, the North London, to reach a City terminus at Broad Street.

The geography of London passenger terminals was both the cause and the result of the different types of suburban traffic carried by the companies. For instance, the GE made no regular use of its connection to the underground Metropolitan line, and any of its passengers wishing to reach the West End had to change trains. This faithfully reflected the higher proportion of lower class traffic on the GE who did not have West End destinations. The only other company which did not provide through trains to both the West End and the City was the LSW. (The tube connection of 1898 has already been mentioned.) This may indicate a high class suburban traffic with an appreciably shorter working day, who were prepared to regard the delights of Surrey as adequate compensation for interrupted journeys to the City.

In contrast with the relative stability of the passenger system, the network of London freight facilities has almost disappeared since the Second World War. Most of the main terminals, such as Nine Elms, Broad Street or Somers Town have been closed, together with the smaller depots which operated alongside the passenger stations. Companies in the Underground Group confined themselves to the provision of passenger services, although the one underground company outside the Group, the Metropolitan, did run freight trains. The main line companies operated a few freight services to depots on underground railways, such as the Midland's goods and coal depot at West Kensington on the District line. This was one of a number of depots owned by the northern companies — the LNW, the Midland and the GN — on the lines of other companies. For instance, in south London, the LNW had a depot at Knights Hill on the LBSC, while on the LCD the GN maintained a yard at Brockley and the Midland had coal drops at Walworth. All were closed after the Second World War, mainly victims of the decline in demand for domestic coal.

Another change with adverse effects on freight traffic over London railways has been the decline to extinction of the London docks system. All the companies except the underground railways, had depots in the port of London, either on the river or in the docks. For example, in the Poplar area, waterside depots were operated by the NL, GE, Midland, GN, LNW, and GW companies. The depots have gone, and the lines that served them survive only if they carry passenger traffic.

The character of the views selected depends not only on where they were taken, but also when. The chronology of London railways, like the geography, is distinctive. On balance, modernization reached London early. For instance, electrification of its local services was virtually completed by the Southern Railway between the wars. At this time, of the rest of the 'Big Four', the LMS operated its own electric trains in the north west, but electrification to east and west was confined to the underground companies. After delay owing to the Second World War, all the LNE suburban routes were electrified with BR or London Transport services, or closed completely. The provision of electric train services in the north east, however, lagged behind south London by about 30 years. Electrification of the underground lines came sooner, the tube lines being electric from the start, with the City and South London being opened in 1890. The sub-surface underground lines operated by the District and the Metropolitan companies were electrified by 1905.

The construction of new lines between the wars was confined to the Southern and to the Underground Group. Although the Southern lines carried freight, construction in the twenties and thirties was particularly associated with the great building boom of the period, with its promise of passenger traffic. On existing lines, some of which had been opened in anticipation of the spread of houses, new stations had been built and in some cases, stations from earlier periods were rebuilt. On the Southern, the cost of providing new stations such as Falconwood and Berrylands was borne partly by speculative builders. The rebuilding of existing stations was assisted by government money, made readily available to combat unemployment — Richmond and Wimbledon are good examples of subsidised stations. On the Underground system, the architectural standard of the new buildings was particularly high, both for the rebuilds, as on the Ealing and South Harrow, or on new lines, such as the extension of the Piccadilly line to Cockfosters. Development was concentrated to the south, west and north, the only major development to the east being the extension of the underground electric trains alongside the existing LMS line to Upminster, on new tracks with some new stations. For the most part, services to the east and north east stagnated, with a 1939 steam hauled train to Chingford not much different from one of 1919, while the gas lit coaches on the

North Woolwich line showed even less change. Only after the Second World War did electrification and modernization reach the north east, and it was not until the 1980s that revival reached the East End. For instance, after the end of first passenger and then freight trains to Poplar, 1987 should see revival, with the trains of the Docklands Light Railway.

The selection of views has been made to illustrate the changing railway scene in different parts of the London area. The choice has been based on objective criteria, but in one or two cases, without departing from the 'rules', it has proved possible to indulge personal bias. For instance, in seeking an example of a rebuilt underground station of the 1930s, the choice of Alperton depended partly on the fact that in 1903, my grandfather, who for many years had been foreman at Sloane Square, went there as Alperton's first station master. The selection of North Woolwich to represent transformation in the dockland area, reflected my dockland upbringing, with early childhood journeys from the long closed station at Tidal Basin on the North Woolwich line. The South Tottenham picture shows myself and members of the London University Extra-Mural Class of 1954-5, exploring the London railways of that time. This group included an assembly of railway expertise, both amateur and professional, which is unlikely to be equalled. Some of them have died, but others are still, like me, fascinated by London railways.

Abbreviations

The descriptions of each of the 48 sites selected are headed with the following information — name of site, identity of railway undertaking associated with the site, grid reference, dates of views and, where applicable, details of station accommodation as listed in the *Railway Clearing Handbook of Stations for 1938*.

The abbreviations for railway undertakings follow the introduction for each of the chapters. Those for station accommodation are as follows –

G   Goods

G★   Coal class, mineral and station to station traffic in truck loads

P   Passengers and parcels

P★   Passengers only

F   Furniture vans, carriages, motor cars, portable engines and machines on wheels

L   Livestock

H   Horse boxes and prize cattle vans

C   Private carriages and motor cars by passenger train.

ONE

Central London

Compared with other parts of the metropolitan area, the railway pattern of central London included more terminals than through stations. Even if, as at King's Cross or Paddington, there were through platforms, these were detached and were for the use of the more local trains. Local and central government policy kept surface railways — and also street tramways — out of the City and West End of London, so that the main line railways terminated, like the spokes of a wheel, around a central zone. The first move to connect them by what came to be known as the Inner Circle, was accomplished by steam railways running mostly underneath roads, sufficiently near the surface to allow some of the smoke to escape. The first section was opened between Paddington and Farringdon in 1863, and was originally operated with Great Western broad gauge trains. The final section, completing the Inner Circle, was opened between Aldgate and Mansion House in 1884. Construction of sub-surface underground lines was extremely expensive, partly because of the interference with other underground services such as water supply and drainage. The technique of constructing tubes with iron segments was well-known: in fact, a tube railway with cable traction was opened under the Thames near the site of the future Tower Bridge in 1870. By 1890, when the City and South London Railway was opened, electric traction was available, and in the period up to the First World War, many of the tube lines within the Inner Circle were constructed. Apart from relatively short links, between the wars tube railway development was concentrated on the fast growing suburban areas to the north and west.

However, after the Second World War, there was a return to central London, with the new Victoria and Jubilee lines.

The main line companies had three cross London routes. However, two of these, the West London and East London routes, were outside the central area. (Although it carried through freight and passenger trains, the East London line ran underground for most of its length.) The section of the Inner Circle between King's Cross and Farringdon did carry through freight and passenger traffic for many years. Passenger traffic ended in 1916, and freight in 1969, but at the time of writing, work is in progress for the restoration of through passenger services. After many years, during which changing between London terminals involved the inconvenience of transfer to the underground system, some through trains were re-introduced on the West London line in 1986.

While passenger traffic carried by the underground lines within central London is increasing, freight has been virtually eliminated. Many of the great freight terminals, such as St. Pancras and Broad Street were closed in the sixties. Smaller goods stations, such as those adjoining Farringdon on the Inner Circle, were closed at various dates between 1936 and 1962. (The closure of the GW depot at Farringdon in 1962 ended the opportunity to see steam locomotives of the Western Region running over the Metropolitan line of 1863.) There have been closures of passenger stations, both on the main lines and the Underground in central London, although in many cases this has been the result of replacement by new stations. Broad Street,

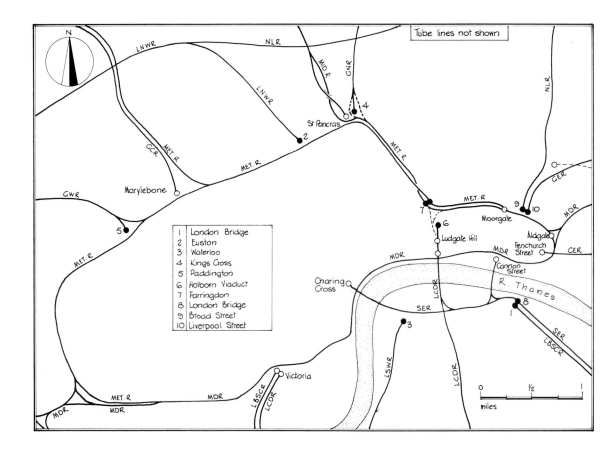

N

Tube lines not shown

LNWR
NLR
MID.R
GNR
NLR
LNWR
St Pancras 2
GCR
MET.R 4
MET.R
MET.R
GWR
Marylebone
GER
MET.R
MDR
5
MET.R 7
9 10
Moorgate
Aldgate
6
Fenchurch Street
Ludgate Hill
MDR
CER
MDR
Cannon Street
R. Thames
Charing Cross
LCDR
SER 8
1
3
SER
LSWR
LBSCR
LCDR
MET.R
MDR
LBSCR
LCDR
Victoria
MDR
MDR

1	London Bridge
2	Euston
3	Waterloo
4	Kings Cross
5	Paddington
6	Holborn Viaduct
7	Farringdon
8	London Bridge
9	Broad Street
10	Liverpool Street

0   ½   1
miles

which for many years has only handled a dwindling local traffic, is the only large passenger station with closure planned in 1986 — its traffic is to be transferred to Liverpool Street. A threat to Marylebone, also suffering from reduced traffic, has been removed. A number of the terminals, including Euston and London Bridge, have undergone radical rebuilding. However, apart from the virtual disappearance of freight traffic, the railway pattern of central London has not changed greatly since the end of the Second World War.

Abbreviations for chapter one

BR(ER)	British Railways (Eastern Region)
BR(LMR)	British Railways (London Midland Region)
BR(SR)	British Railways (Southern Region)
BR(WR)	British Railways (Western Region)
GCR	Great Central Railway
GER	Great Eastern Railway
GNR	Great Northern Railway
GWR	Great Western Railway
LBSCR	London, Brighton and South Coast Railway
LCDR	London Chatham and Dover Railway
LMSR	London Midland and Scottish Railway
LNER	London and North Eastern Railway
LNWR	London and North Western Railway
LPTB	London Passenger Transport Board
LSWR	London and South Western Railway
LRT	London Regional Transport
LTB	London Transport Board
LTE	London Transport Executive
MDR	Metropolitan District Railway
MET.R.	Metropolitan Railway
MID.R.	Midland Railway
NLR	North London Railway
SR	Southern Railway
SER	South Eastern Railway
SECR	South Eastern and Chatham Managing Committee

Undertakings in bold lettering in the main took over from the original companies. For the main lines there were two stages: they were taken over by the 'Big Four' in 1923 and then by British Railways in 1948. For the underground railways, there was a principal stage — the 'Take over' by the LPTB in 1933. (This was succeeded in turn by LTE, LTB, LTE and LRT.)

1 London Bridge Station LBSCR/SR/BR(SR) PFHC
c 1905/7 October 1972/3 April 1986 TQ 328803

The London and Greenwich was London's first railway and London Bridge its first terminal station. Unlike many of the terminals which followed, it did not take its name from a district or thoroughfare, but from the nearby bridge leading into the City of London. This is entirely appropriate, as a high proportion of its passengers have always been on their way to and from work across the bridge. With each extension of the railway, the number of passengers increased. After the opening to Greenwich in 1838, Croydon was reached in 1839, Brighton in 1841 and Dover in 1844. The terminal facilities were shared by the South Eastern and the London, Brighton and South Coast Companies, who in 1844 opened a new building for their joint use. Traffic continued to expand — 625,000 passengers used London Bridge in 1846 and 10.8 million in 1854. The joint station proved inadequate and unsatisfactory and it was replaced by two separate terminals, that for the SE being completed in 1851 and the LBSC in 1854.

Traffic continued to grow, but from the 1860s London Bridge had to share its traffic with other terminals. From 1860 LBSC passengers for the West End could use the new station at Victoria,

London Bridge Station 1905

London Bridge Station 1972

London Bridge Station 1986

while the SE opened Charing Cross for the West End in 1864 and Cannon Street for the City in 1866. Another development, the arrival of the London, Chatham and Dover Railway, also reduced the London Bridge share of the rising total. This did not prevent it from becoming one of the busiest stations in London, with an average peak of 94,400 passengers a day in 1967, although this had fallen to 68,700 a day in 1983. There is a sad coincidence in the decline of traffic and the rebuilding of the station in the 1970s.

When the first photograph was taken, about 1905, although London Bridge was mainly a station for commuters, it was also used by the local population for day excursions to the seaside or, in the season, to the hopfields of Kent. However, the number of horse buses and cabs in the station forecourt indicates arrivals and departures by other types of passenger. One side of the facade of the SE station of 1851 was demolished to make way for the extension to Charing Cross, but a corner of the surviving section appears on the extreme left. Canopies protected the entrances to both the SE and LBSC stations. On the right is the hotel of 1861, designed by Henry Currey, who was also responsible for the Victorian St. Thomas's Hospital. The London Bridge clientele was unlikely to support a hotel, and in 1893 it was sold to the LBSC who used it for office accommodation. About two-thirds of the facade of the LBSC terminal of 1854 appears; this is indicated by the proportion of the parapet, bearing the title of the 'London, Brighton and South Coast Railway' which appears in this view.

The photograph of 1972 records the effects of war damage, and demolition preceding the rebuilding of the 1970s. In the forecourt, it can be seen that cars have replaced the horse bus and cabs. (The comparative rarity of taxis at London Bridge reflects its patronage.) The hotel and the top storey of the station were virtually destroyed in the air raids of 29 and 30 December 1940, and were subsequently demolished. The position of the rusticated pilasters and quoins facilitates

comparison of the 1905 and 1972 photographs. The view of 1986, records the complete obliteration of the Victorian buildings, by the new station, formally opened by the Bishop of Southwark in 1978, although work was not finally completed until 1979. Buses still use the forecourt, which now has a roof. The only feature from the past is the iron pillar, supporting the SE extension line to Charing Cross.

2 Euston LNWR/LMSR/BR(LMR) PFHC
1960/22 April 1967/3 April 1986 TQ 297826

Opened in 1836, London Bridge was the first of London's railway termini, but Euston, opened in 1837, was the first station to serve a main line. It is not entirely coincidental that the earlier stations are those which have undergone the most radical rebuilding. In 1837, the train shed at Euston was felt to be too inadequate to form a gateway to the route to the Midlands, the North and to Scotland, and so the directors commissioned the erection of a magnificent Doric portico, completed in 1838. The other main feature of the old Euston was the Great Hall of 1849, the finest waiting room in London. In contrast, modest wooden platforms were added over the years, and by the 1930s, the case for radical reconstruction was clear. The intention to rebuild was announced by Sir Josiah Stamp (later Lord Stamp), president of the LMS in 1933, and by 1938 detailed plans had been formulated. The Second World War prevented their fulfilment, and it was not until 1959 that BR announced new plans for Euston. They came at a time when BR was desperately anxious to promote an image of modernity, and mainly for this reason, in 1961, the portico was sacrificed. In the same vein, the new circulating area which was the nearest thing to a replacement for the Great Hall, had the atmosphere of an airport rather than a railway station. The new Euston was opened by the Queen in 1968.

Euston Station 1960

Euston Station 1967 (*above*)   Euston Station 1986 (*below*)

The first view was taken in 1960, before rebuilding had begun. Many Victorian railway developments reflect the spur of competition, and after the opening of the new Midland Railway terminus at St. Pancras, the LNW acquired a wide strip of ground between their hotel and the Euston Road and constructed an impressive approach drive. The entrance was flanked by two pavilions, which appear in all three views and were opened in 1870. They were both used at various times, their functions including a parcels office, a post office and the office of a travel agent. On the corners of each of them were inscribed, in alphabetical order, a list of the principal towns reached by the LNW company in 1870. The lists, preserved in stone, give a vivid, if rather false, impression of the extent of the LNW 'empire', as some of the places mentioned could only be reached from Euston by the most intrepid travellers with time to spare, a liking for changing trains at unlikely junctions and an intimate knowledge of Bradshaw. A choice of doubtful claims, selecting one from each of the eight corners, might include Bedford, Cambridge, Derby, Hereford, Leicester, Oxford, Peterborough and Swansea. In between the pavilions, the first two views show a statue of Robert Stephenson, engineer of the London and Birmingham Railway. This was a bronze statue by Baron Carlo Marochetti, presented to the LNW by the Institution of Civil Engineers, to whom it has been returned. Beyond, all three views show the war memorial, erected in memory of the 3719 men of the LNW who lost their lives in the First World War.

At the back of the 1960 view is the Euston Hotel. The great period for building hotels at the London termini was the 1860s; the Euston Hotel, opened in 1839, was the first. As frequently happened, it was opened by a satellite company, in this case the London and Birmingham Hotel and Dormitories Company. It reflected the closeness of the coaching era, both in the similiarity of its function to that of the coaching inn and also in its class distinctions, with two separate buildings — the Euston, on the east side (right hand side of the photograph) for first class passengers and the Victoria, on the opposite side of the road, for others. As shown in the view, the western side suffered war damage. Although Euston was the first of the railway hotels, in its original form it was left far behind in luxury by those of the 1850s and 1860s. This was remedied in 1881 when a new central block over the roadway was completed, and the two original blocks were brought up to the standard of the Midland Grand. It blocked the view of the portico from the Euston Road, but was well patronised until its closure in 1963. By the time of the second view, in 1967, demolition was complete and new construction in hand; by 1986, the new Euston was already 18 years old.

3 Waterloo LSWR/SR/BR(SR) PHC
c 1948/3 April 1986 TQ 310796

Like London Bridge Station, Waterloo was sited on the south side of the Thames near the approach to a bridge, and until 1882, was called Waterloo Bridge Station. Unlike London Bridge, it was better placed for the West End, rather than the City. A significant proportion of London Bridge traffic was siphoned off by the extension to Charing Cross, but there was no corresponding development at Waterloo. (A connection to the line between London Bridge and Charing Cross was provided in 1864 but saw little use.) Of greater importance for access to the City was the opening of the self-contained Waterloo and City tube line in 1898.

In a few cases, London termini have been re-sited in better positions, including the present Paddington and Liverpool Street. Waterloo was the first example, replacing the original London and Southampton terminus at Nine Elms in 1848. As at Euston, the additional platforms contributed to increasing difficulties

Waterloo Station 1948

Waterloo Station 1986

for passengers and staff, and in 1901 the Chief Engineer of the LSW went to study terminals in the U.S.A. Preliminary work on the site had begun in 1900, but paced by the availability of finance and delayed by the Great War, rebuilding took over 20 years; the formal opening of the new Waterloo by Queen Mary thus took place in 1922. Subsequent changes have been cosmetic rather than basic, including a new ticket office, arrival and departure indicators and a new floor for the concourse.

Stations are essentially interfaces between rail and road, or rail and rail. The means by which passengers reach or leave a station, although not the direct concern of the railway authorities, are of great importance for the smooth working of a station. Unlike London Bridge, Waterloo has never had an extensive forecourt, and many buses, rather than terminating, call at stops in the adjoining York and Waterloo Roads. For taxi cabs and motor cars, and later, Red Arrow bus services, special facilities were provided at Waterloo.

These are shown in views taken in 1948 and 1986. As part of the station reconstruction scheme, in 1911 a roadway was constructed from the Westminster Bridge Road, passing under the approach viaduct to the station, and following the south side to reach the booking office. The roadway could also be reached from York Street and Lower Marsh. In 1922 it was extended to York Road, and a one way traffic flow was instituted. When the 1948 view was taken, the name of the London and South Western company was still engraved in stone above the entrance; the indication that it led to Waterloo had been added by the Southern Railway. The 1986 view shows the way in which BR have both covered the name of the old company and also provided comparable information. Being railway property the entrance to the roadway was provided with iron gates, and these appear in both views. In the right background, the truss of the railway viaduct is visible, and the white glazed tiles facing the brick abutment. Clearly

visible in the 1986 view, but indistinct in that of 1948, is the side of the Waterloo signal box, which replaced manually operated points and signals with electric control. Externally, it has remained unchanged since 1936, but a new control panel went into commission in 1984. The most striking change in the road is the removal of the tram lines, incorporating the London system of live rails reached through a slot placed between the running rails. The car shown is on route 33 from West Norwood to Finsbury Park (Manor House), closed in 1951. A pre-war taxi is shown passing the tram and may be compared with the modern taxi shown in the 1986 view.

4 King's Cross GNR/LNER/BR(ER) PFLHC
26 November 1950/27 August 1958/23 October 1971/3 April 1986 TQ 304833

The Great Northern Railway reached London before its permanent terminal was ready. It was London's second main route to the North, and formed the southern section of the east coast main line to Scotland, breaking the monopoly of the west coast route from Euston. The section from London to Peterborough was opened in 1850, but it wasn't until 1852 that the two great train sheds, which formed the London terminus, were ready for use. All the other arched train sheds — at St. Pancras, Paddington, Charing Cross and Cannon Street — were masked by hotels, but at King's Cross the hotel was built to one side and the outline of the arches dominate the facade of the station. In 1858, the traffic from the Midland Railway, which had been fed on to the Euston route at Rugby, was captured by the GN and joined its line at Hitchin. This arrangement continued for ten years, until the Midland opened their own London extension to St. Pancras. However, because of the development of suburbs in North London, King's Cross traffic increased so much that the adjoining local station was opened in 1874, and enlarged in 1895.

King's Cross Station 1950

King's Cross Station 1958

In the 1860s, in anticipation of the growth of commuter traffic, communication with the City was developed, and the GN opened an underground extension to join the Metropolitan Railway. This gave access to the City, on to the LCDR and later to the SE. It was closed in 1976. Passengers changing to underground trains, were provided with a subway to the Metropolitan line station in 1892, to what became the Piccadilly line in 1906 and the Northern line in 1907. Major developments, including the construction of the present ticket and inquiry offices, came in 1973, followed by the electrification of the outer suburban services in 1976.

The views selected for King's Cross concentrate on changes in trains rather than buildings. The first view was taken on a foggy Sunday morning in November 1950. The famous Great Northern Atlantics, designed by H.A. Ivatt could be seen at King's Cross, with main line express trains, for many years. By March 1950, the last survivor in normal service was based at Grantham Shed and was due for withdrawal. Great Northern No.294 was built at Doncaster works in 1905, and had become in succession, LNER No.3294, LNER No.2822 and finally BR No.62822. It was decided that instead of merely being laid aside, 62822's final run should be on a special express train from King's Cross to Doncaster, and the first photograph records the event. After about 25 years, Pacifics designed by Sir Nigel Gresley, replaced Atlantics, and with some modifications, continued to work principal express trains out of King's Cross until they were ousted by diesel traction. The second photograph shows *Neil Gow*, built at Doncaster works in 1924 as LNER No.2581, later LNER, No.82 and finally BR No. 60082. *Neil Gow* was rebuilt with a higher pressure boiler in 1943 and was withdrawn in 1963. On the platform are numerous hand-propelled trolleys, which were used for the movement of parcels and mail carried on passenger trains. The track consists of standard rail held in chairs and supported on wooden sleepers. The signal box, colour light signals and point motors, were provided in 1932. The 1971 view shows the same signal box, but steam has been displaced by diesel traction. There were 22 locomotives of the Deltic class and they 'reigned' at King's Cross from their

King's Cross Station 1971

King's Cross Station 1986

introduction in 1961 until their replacement by High Speed Trains in 1978. With their 3300 HP Napier engines, they were among the most popular locomotives on British Rail, and made 100mph (161kmph) running on the east coast main line a regular event. The extent of their popularity is reflected in the preservation of no less than five of the class. During the era of the Deltics, locomotives and coaches continued to be separate units, but with the advent of the high speed train, two locomotives, known as power cars, were permanently attached to a set of coaches. With one power car at each end, turnround at terminals became simpler, and the track layout at King's Cross was modified. The final view shows the end of power car No.43104, built at Crewe works and named *County of Cleveland*. Apart from the trains, other changes include the replacement of the signal box in 1971 and electrification in 1976. At present, only suburban services are electrically operated, but work on the east coast mainline electrification is in progress, and by the end of the 1980s, King's Cross will be occupied almost exclusively by electric traction.

5 Paddington GWR/BR(WR) GPFLHC
c 1905/25 March 1986 TQ 266812

At one stage, the Great Western contemplated sharing Euston with the LNW, which would have produced a two company station like Victoria or London Bridge. In the event the adoption of a broad gauge and other factors, determined the GW to open their own station at Paddington. Like the LSW and the GE, the GW paused before advancing to its final terminal — in its case from 1838 until 1854. The permanent station was the second London terminus to have a magnificent glazed arched roof, which it still retains. Important alterations and additions were made between 1911 and 1916, and again, subsidised by government loans, between 1930 and 1934, but at

Paddington Station 1905

neither stage was the essential character of Paddington impaired. At many London stations, the design of the hotel may be attributed to an architect and the train shed to an engineer, but the train shed at Paddington was the result of co-operation between Isambard Kingdom Brunel and his friend, Matthew Digby Wyatt. *The Illustrated London News* for 8 July 1854, refers to 'the joint work of Mr Brunel and Mr M.D.Wyatt, the former having arranged the general plan and the engineering and business portion; the latter the architectural details in every department'.

Observing the success of the railway hotel at Euston, the GW was associated with the satellite company which opened a hotel across the end of the train sheds in 1854. Although there was a major extension at the rear, completed in 1936, the facade on Praed Street has changed little. The hotel was designed by P.C. Hardwick with details by John Thomas. The most striking of the details was the high relief in the pediment showing

Paddington Station 1986

hotel the end of one of the train sheds can just be seen, with their elaborate ironwork. The streets remain unpaved, and lit by gas lamps; the horse cabs waiting outside the hotel may be associated with the orderly bin at the end of Eastbourne Terrace. The gap at the back of the hotel was filled by a new office building in a traditional style, completed in 1933. The 1986 view shows few changes in the facade of the hotel. However, most striking is the new entrance canopy, adorned with shrubs. Above it there were some elaborately carved supports for a balcony, but these were replaced by rather agressively plain stonework, incorporating the letters 'GWR' in the form of a monogram. These changes were accompanied by internal reconstruction, completed in 1938. Even with these alterations, with the exception of the Midland Grand, the Great Western Hotel presents the most striking facade of any of the London railway hotels.

Britannia surrounded by representations of Peace, Plenty, Industry and Science. A contemporary account refers to the 'French style of Louis XIV or later — the curved roof forms are a startling novelty here . . .'. Stops at each end of the facade were provided by towers, surmounted by pierced parapets and curved spires, and, somewhat surprisingly, chimneys.

The view of 1905 shows the hotel virtually as built, at that time with 103 bedrooms. It is noteworthy that all the windows on one side of the tower are unglazed. Beyond the back of the

6 Holborn Viaduct **LCDR/SECR/SR/BR(SR)** **P**
1913/20 August 1955/1 April 1967/3 April 1986
TQ 317813

The London, Chatham and Dover Railway was a latecomer to London, constructed over 20 years later than the other three southern companies. However, like the Brighton and South Eastern companies, it needed London commuter traffic, and therefore well placed London stations were essential. Also, like the other two companies, in the 1860s the LCD sought stations for both the West End and the City. Victoria, its West End terminal was reached in 1862, but access to the City took longer. By 1862, the line had reached Elephant and Castle; by 1864 it had crossed the river to a station at Ludgate Hill; and in 1866 it was extended to join the underground line of the Metropolitan Railway. Trains could then run through to the Great Northern or Midland lines.

Holborn Viaduct 1913

Holborn Viaduct 1955

Holborn Viaduct 1967

The two LCD stations, Blackfriars Bridge, which was south of the river, and Ludgate Hill, were both through stations of modest capacity, and by the 1870s, traffic had grown to an extent which merited a terminus for the main line trains. These served both City and the West End by means of division or joining according to direction, at the junction at Herne Hill.

The cost of the site of Holborn Viaduct terminus was high, but some money was saved by providing short platforms. This was possible because of the arrangement of combining or dividing trains at Herne Hill, so that Holborn Viaduct did not need to accommodate full length trains. Changes in traffic patterns left Holborn Viaduct with local rather than main line trains; because of decreased demand three platform faces were lengthened, leaving the other three unusable for normal passenger trains. In addition to the platforms at viaduct level, others were opened on the connection to the Metropolitan, named Snow Hill until 1912, and then Holborn Viaduct (Low Level). Passenger services on the through line finished in 1916 and freight services in 1969. Work began in 1986 to restore this link.

Of the four views of Holborn Viaduct, three were taken from approximately the same position on the island platform, 4/5, and one was taken from a train standing in the side platform, 1. The first, of 1913, shows the station virtually as built. All the termini north of the Thames, except Broad Street and Fenchurch Street with their short distance traffic, acquired hotels; Holborn Viaduct was no exception. The rear of the hotel building of 1877 appears in the background. It was requisitioned by the government during the First World War and then let to W.T. Henleys Telegraph Works Company. In 1941 it was damaged by aerial bombardment, and gutted by fire in the same year. Holborn Viaduct was not provided with one of the magnificent arched roofs, but had three spans of ridged roof with iron trusses. Even these did not extend for the full length of the platforms, protection being extended by veranda-type canopies. Two gas

lamps are visible on platforms 2 and 3, in the centre of the photograph, with electric lamps, suspended from signal posts at platforms 1 and 4 and 5. Water cranes, for steam locomotives are provided at the ends of each platform; these would have been fed from the large water tank adjoining platform 1. The semaphore signal on platform 1 is partly obscured, but those for 2 and 3 are clearly visible. Finally, a porter's trolley on platform 4 and 5 carries a destination board for a coach to Dover.

The island platform 4/5 was lengthened to take eight coach electric trains in 1925; platform 1 was similarly lengthened in 1939. Electric trains ran into Holborn Viaduct from 1925, but the third live rail was only provided at platforms long enough to accomodate them. This is shown in the view of 1955. At this time steam locomotives were still in use for the parcels vans, and the water cranes and the large tank remained in position. However, new electric lighting had been installed. Parcels vans are to be seen at platform 2/3 and electric trains occupy platforms 1 and 5. The train at 5 includes a former LBSC coach, and a Bulleid coach of the type added to three car electric sets after the War. The aftermath of bomb damage shows in the fibrous panels, which have replaced wood at the ends of the overall roof, and in the ruins of the hotel. The Victorian hotel and station buildings were replaced by new structures in 1963, and these are shown in the view taken in 1967. At this time, the original roofing was being removed but there were remains of the roof trusses of the overall roof, and of the canopies which had provided cover for the outer ends of the platforms. The end of steam locomotives had led to the removal of the water cranes and water tank; the vans shown on platform 6 would have been moved by a diesel locomotive. All three full length platforms were occupied by electric trains with four coach units at platform 4/5 and an eight coach unit at platform 1. They all belong to the S.R. 4 EPB type (BR Class 415/1) introduced in 1951 and built at Eastleigh; in 1967 they were painted green. Only

Holborn Viaduct 1986

short distance services were operated from Holborn Viaduct, and set 5207 at platform 4 carries the headcode 83 for the Holborn Viaduct to Sevenoaks service.

The view of 1986 shows that all the original platform roofing has been replaced by rather short, modern canopies. Platform 2/3 was removed in 1973. New lamps are in position, but the two eight coach trains in the station are of the same 4-EPB type as appeared in the 1967 view, although now painted in standard BR grey and blue livery instead of southern green. The only clear relic of the Victorian station is the base of the water tank of platform 1. Holborn Viaduct belongs to a period of extreme railway competition, and could be a casualty of rationalisation.

7 Farringdon Met.R/LPTB/LTE/LTB/LRT P*
23 August 1947/3 April 1986 TQ 316819

The drive to reach the City by virtually all the main line companies in the 1860s has already been noted. With the network of streets in the built up areas, railway lines had to be elevated on viaducts or depressed into tunnels, and north of the Thames, most of the new lines ran below ground level. The Metropolitan Railway was particularly associated with the Great Western, and was opened from a junction just outside Paddington to Farringdon in 1863, with mixed gauge tracks. Extensions followed to Aldersgate (now Barbican) in 1865, to Liverpool Street in 1875 and to Aldgate in 1876. The central section, between Kings Cross and Farringdon, received a great increase of traffic in 1866, when it was connected to the LCD at the Farringdon end. A link to the newly opened Midland Station at St. Pancras was completed in 1868. In the same year, the line between Kings Cross and Farringdon was duplicated with what was, in effect, a separate double track railway.

Railway lore enshrines Carlisle as being the station where the greatest variety of the trains of pregrouping companies could be seen. There it was possible to see trains from six companies but Farringdon, from 1880 until 1899, offered seven. On the new line of 1868 there were trains of the GN, Midland, LCD and SE companies, and on the original line, those of the GW, Metropolitan and Metropolitan District companies. The up track

Farringdon 1947

of the Widened Lines was electrified on the low
tension live rail system between the wars. The
original tracks were electrified on a low tension
live rail system in 1905, and the 'new' tracks,
known as the Widened Lines, were electrified on
the 25 KV overhead wire system in 1982. As well
as the considerable through passenger and goods
traffic, there was that to the nearby goods
terminals — the GN (1874-1956), the GW (1869-

1962), the Midland (1878-1936), and the
Metropolitan's own (1909-36).

The two views were taken on the Widened
Lines, which in Farringdon Station are at a lower
level than the original railway. Farringdon
retains its two-span overall roof with the usual
Metropolitan arrangement of a concourse
reached from a footbridge spanning the four
tracks. The centre platform is reached by a free-
standing, wide stairway, but in order to avoid
using platform space, the stairways to the side
platforms are set back behind the side walls. In

Farringdon 1986

1947, the platforms on the Widened Lines were still wooden but an even more interesting survival was the station name board on the left.

The name 'Farringdon and High Holborn' replaced 'Farringdon Street' in 1922, and was, in turn, replaced by 'Farringdon' in 1936. Perhaps because the Widened Lines were out of use for passengers during the Second World War, the previous name board was not altered and bears the old name with the red, lozenge background used by the Metropolitan. In fact, although the view was taken in 1947, there were no significant changes from the 1930s. The locomotive, with its condensing equipment for underground working, was originally 2-6-2T No.15534, designed by Fowler and built at Derby for the LMS in 1931. It was renumbered in 1934 to 35 and by BR to 40035, before its withdrawal in 1961. The coaches are from ex-Midland compartment stock. The 1986 view shows the wooden platform replaced by concrete and asphalt, and the wooden dividing wall between the two sides of the station replaced by brickwork. A standard LT station name board has replaced that of the Metropolitan Railway. But perhaps the most striking change, is that of the train, electric multiple unit No.317306 of BR class 317, built in York in 1981. It is shown running in, on the 14.50 from Moorgate to Luton.

8 London Bridge Station   SER/SECR/SR/ BR(SR) PFHC
1913/13 March 1977 TQ 332802

The background history of London Bridge has already been given. The previous views recorded the changes in the exterior of the station; the views of 1913 and 1977 show platforms and trains. Both views were taken at the country end of the through platforms, used since 1864 by SE trains going on to Charing Cross or Cannon Street. There was a widening on the northern side, the right hand side of the photograph, in

1893-4, with both an additional platform and the SE offices in Tooley Street. Although the track re-arrangements and the re-signalling of the 1970s increased the traffic capacity of the through station, there has been no fundamental change in the arrangement of the three island platforms since the 1890s.

Comparing 1913 and 1977, in both cases steel rails are carried in chairs on wooden sleepers, but from 1926 a third rail, carrying electric current was added. In 1913, points were moved by rodding, but in 1977 they were operated by electric motors placed under the ramp at the end of the platform. (The box adjoining the left hand track in the 1913 view housed a detonator placer for use when a combination of semaphore signals and London 'pea soup' fogs made the running of trains a difficult task.) The semaphore signals in the earlier view were first replaced in 1928. The platforms have been extended and this is indicated by the demarcation between stone coping and flagstones, and concrete and asphalt, visible in the 1977 view. An open footbridge was replaced by a much wider enclosed bridge in 1975, while the gas lamps of 1913 contrast with the electric lights of 1977.

A number of corresponding features appear in both views, including the platform awnings with their decorative vallance, the wall and railings and the railway offices, with their conspicuous stonework. A striking change is the removal of the large enamel plates proclaiming the merits of Pears soap, removed from a building adjoining the railway. The train of 1913 was on its way by the SE route to Margate, via Ashford and Ramsgate. The typical SEC coaches were drawn by locomotive No.217. This was built at Ashford works in 1898, rebuilt to class B1 in 1910, and withdrawn in 1950. The train of 1977 was running from Cannon Street via the loop line to Dartford and consisted of ten electrically powered coaches. The leading two coach unit was followed by two four coach units, all built in the early 1950s. Unit 5703 belonged to the Southern Region's 2-EPB class (BR class 416/2) introduced in 1951 and constructed at Eastleigh Works.

London Bridge Station 1913

London Bridge Station 1977

9 Broad Street Station NLR/LMSR/BR(LMR) P
22 February 1964/6 March 1976 TQ 332817

Of all the railway sites chosen for this book, Broad Street is the saddest. A number of stations, such as London Bridge, have suffered a decline in traffic, but Broad Street is the only London terminal, which, by the time this book appears, will have been closed and demolished. It was very much a London station, with few of its trains passing far beyond the Greater London area. (For a brief period, from 1910 to 1915, there was a Monday to Friday express to Birmingham and Wolverhampton.) Reflecting the short journeys and lack of passenger luggage, Broad Street

Broad Street Station 1964

Broad Street Station 1976

platforms shared the distinction with Fenchurch Street and Blackfriars of being accessible by stairways only. When the Central London tube line was extended in 1912 a lift was added to the Broad Street concourse.

The North London Railway began as a ring route, linking the LNW main line to the docks of East London. However, it soon began to carry passengers to the City by using part of the London and Blackwall Railway, to reach Fenchurch Street. This extremely circuitous route was greatly improved upon in 1865, when a branch was built from the ring route to a new London terminus at Broad Street. Because of its short distance traffic, the new station did not attract an hotel, but the highly decorated terminal buildings obscured the ends of the two train sheds, and the elaborate iron work which supported the roofs. In 1875 the LNW and North London trains were joined by those from the GN, a service which ran until November 1976. By the turn of the century, Broad Street was at the height of its importance, being used by about 50,000 passengers during peak periods. Then came competition from electric tram, tube and motor bus, and Broad Street's traffic slumped. In 1968, the number of people using the railway fell to about 9000 passengers on normal weekdays. In 1985, outside peak hours, the service from Richmond, which had for so many years been the mainstay of Broad Street traffic, was diverted over the newly electrified line to North Woolwich. Demolition of the buildings has now begun, and trains use a temporary platform reached by a footway which runs alongside Liverpool Street Station. When a connection is completed at Hackney, trains will run from the North London line into Liverpool Street.

The first view was taken at lunchtime on a Saturday in February 1964. At this time, the eight platform faces, within the original walls, plus a ninth built in 1913 outside the western wall (off right hand side of the photograph), were all in use. Electric services, on the live rail low tension system, were inaugurated to Richmond in 1916, to Watford via Hampstead Heath (peak hours only) in 1917, and finally to Watford via Primrose Hill in 1922. The platforms on the western side — 5 to 9 — were provided with third and fourth rails. No. 1 to 4 were used by steam trains, mainly for the services to Poplar and to destinations on the GN. Between 1923 and 1935 a few trains from the LTS line ran into Broad Street during peak periods. The Poplar service ended in 1944, so that by the time of this view, the former steam lines were only being used by the peak hour services for the GN line. By 1964, the number of people working on Saturday mornings in the City had declined, and this is reflected in the short train in platform 2. On the electric lines one of the three coach sets built at Eastleigh in 1957 and 1958 was about to leave platform 7 for Watford. Although not visible in the photograph, by this time, the business of the station was carried out in two small buildings erected on the concourse in 1957.

When the final view was taken in 1976, Broad Street had been much reduced. During 1967 and 1968 the outer ends of the train sheds were removed, and in 1969, platforms 1, 2, 3 and 9 were abandoned. The remaining platforms — 4, 5, 6, 7 and 8 — were renumbered from 1 to 5. An economy was achieved in 1970 by the removal of the fourth rail on the electrified tracks. Like the 1964 view, that of 1976 was taken at a Saturday lunch time, with platform 4 (formerly 7) occupied by two two-coach diesel units, forming the 12.04 departure for Hertford North. This service was discontinued in 1976 when the GN suburban services were electrified. The two 3-coach electric units at Platform 2 were forming the 12.14 train for Richmond. The trains were of the same type as those seen 12 years earlier, but the station had gone some way down the path to demolition.

10 Liverpool Street Station   GER/LNER/ BR(ER) PHC
17 May 1947/3 April 1986 TQ 333816 and TQ 333818

Few London terminals are at ground level; the elevation of the former Broad Street, above ground level contrasted with Liverpool Street's depression below the surface. The original Eastern Counties line of 1840 crossed East London on a viaduct, comparable to those used by the lines in south London, and to correspond, its terminus at Shorditch was elevated. However, when the extension to Liverpool Street was opened in 1874, construction costs were saved by building it below ground level. Whether this was a good economic decision is arguable, as it involved all trains in the expense of surmounting a 1 in 70 gradient to reach the viaduct. The fact that the extension to Liverpool Street was completed in 1874, rather than in the great extension period of the 1860s, did not detract from a rapid development of traffic. So great was this that by 1894, a second building, increasing the number of platforms from 10 to 18, was added. Most of the London traffic was to the

Liverpool Street Station 1947

eastern and north eastern suburbs, although for limited periods the LBSC and SE collaborated with services to south London via the East London line. Although major changes are now in progress, until recently, apart from the electrification of train services, Liverpool Street did not change greatly, and this is reflected in the views of 1947 and 1986.

Both views show platforms 1, 2 and 3. From 1875 the tracks between platforms 1 and 2 were extended to join the Metropolitan line, but regular services were short-lived; in 1904 the last train to use the connection was a somewhat incredible Metropolitan Railway excursion train from Aylesbury to Yarmouth. Since then, the platforms have been devoted to suburban traffic, and the trains of both 1947 and 1986 were bound for Enfield Town. Perhaps the most striking feature of the first view is the way in which, faced with a 1 in 70 incline, the locomotive had built up

a sufficient head of steam to raise the safety valves; the strength of the exhaust steam indicates an open regulator for maximum acceleration. The need for the roof height of Victorian train sheds, to dispel smoke and steam, is well demonstrated. The roof trusses at Liverpool Street incorporate decorative iron work in the spandrels, obscured by soot in the steam period view.

Locomotive No.7235 of the 2-4-2 T F6 class was built to the design of S.D. Holden at the GE Stratford works in 1911. Its GE number was 6, and it was renumbered by the LNE, first to 7006 then to 7235. BR withdrew the locomotive, which had become their 67235 in 1956 when it had completed 45 years' service. The GE used air brakes, and the Westinghouse air pump, visible on the offside of the locomotive, would have contributed to the characteristic sounds of Liverpool Street in its steam period. GE suburban coaches were austere four wheelers, but in 1925 the LNE introduced five-coach articulated sets known as quintuplets — these appear on both the

Liverpool Street Station 1986

trains in the 1947 photograph. (The figure '3' on the doors indicates third class compartments.) Locomotives did not run round their trains at Liverpool Street. The normal procedure was for a locomotive on an up train to wait until the coaches, provided with a fresh locomotive, left with the next down train. It would then proceed beyond the end of the platform, ready to take out another train; in the 1947 view, an N7 class locomotive, after the departure of the train it brought in, is returning to the end of the platform. A feature of many stations at the time was the type of platform trolley seen on the right of the photograph.

The 1947 view was taken from near the end of platform 4, looking towards the buffers, but the 1986 view faced the opposite direction from steps leading down to platforms 2 and 3. The 14.39 for Enfield Town consisted of one of the class 315 units, introduced in 1980 and built at York. When the platforms on this side of the station were first electrified in 1960, the overhead wires carried 6.25 KV but in 1980 this was raised to 25 KV, to enable the class 315 units to be used. The beam, carrying the lights and platform numbers, obscured the destination board, but the names of some of the stations to be served are visible — Bethnal Green, Cambridge Heath . . . Bruce Grove, White Hart Lane, Silver Street, Lower Edmonton — all very much belonging to the north eastern suburbs of London.

TWO

North and West of London

The area to the north and west of London was penetrated by main lines early in the railway era. These were the lines to Birmingham and to Bristol, and at one stage there was a possibility of them sharing a London terminal. However, Brunel's selection of a broad gauge was one of the reasons for the Great Western building its own terminus at Paddington. The section of the London and Birmingham (later part of the London and North Western system) at the London end was opened in 1837, and the Great Western followed in 1838. There was then a pause in railway construction until the mid-Victorian period. The Great Western acquired short branch lines to Uxbridge and Brentford, but there was also a third main line, the Midland Railway's London extension reaching St. Pancras in 1868. None of the three great companies showed much inclination to develop suburban traffic in rural Middlesex, their efforts being confined to a sprinkling of stations on their main line, and in the case of the GW, two short branches. Meanwhile, both the population and the railway networks of South and of East London grew apace.

Development came to the north west, not initially from the main line companies, but from the London underground railways, seeking passengers to feed on to their expensive central sections. The Metropolitan was the first, its line of 1880 constructed with the double aims of promoting commuter traffic, and also of providing an entry into London for a fourth main line, the Great Central. This was followed by the Metropolitan District, with its extensions to Hounslow in 1883 and to Harrow in 1903. The

original two main lines responded by opening new stations and new lines. The Great Western's new line, by Greenford and Northolt, not only served Middlesex, but also formed part of a more direct route into London used by the main line expresses to Birmingham and the West Midlands. Frequently the trains came before the people, and, in *Summoned by Bells* John Betjeman writes of

. . . dim forgotten stations, wooden shacks
 On oil-lit flimsy platforms among fields
As yet unbuilt-on, deep in Middlesex . . .

The most dramatic growth period was the 1930s when the green meadows of Middlesex disappeared under a sea of suburban housing. No new railways were built — they were there already — but stations were rebuilt, and on some of the underground lines, tube trains replaced those of the Metropolitan and Metropolitan District lines. South London and East London remained closely associated with main line companies, but railway passengers in the north and west were more likely to be carried by underground trains, emerging from the darkness of their tunnels or tubes into what had been the open country of Middlesex.

Abbreviations

BR(LMR)	British Railways (London Midland Region)
BR(WR)	British Railways (Western Region)
CLR	Central London Railway

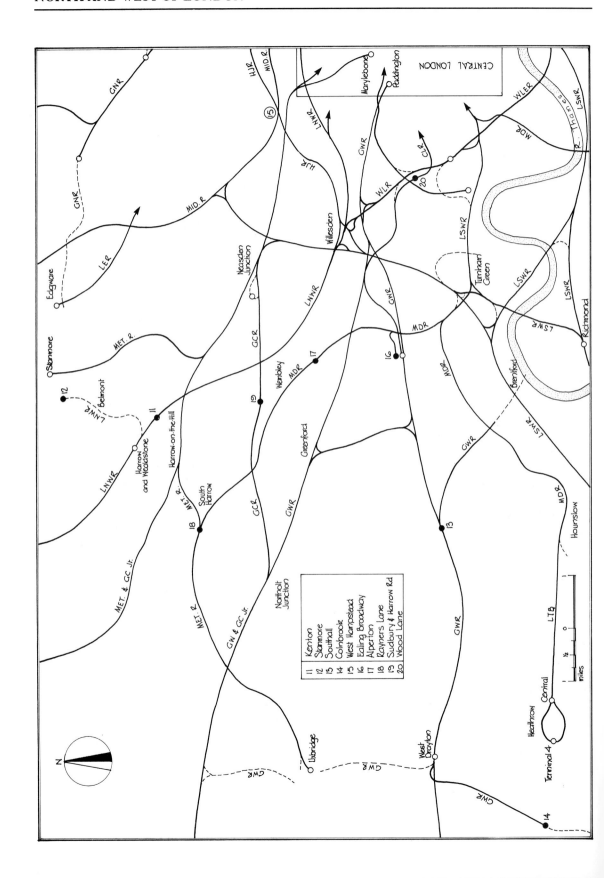

GCR	Great Central Railway
GNR	Great Northern Railway
GWR	Great Western Railway
GW&GC Jt	Great Western and Great Central Joint
HJR	Hampstead Junction Railway (LNWR)
LER	London Electric Railway
LMSR	London, Midland and Scottish Railway
LNER	London and North Eastern Railway
LNWR	London and North Western Railway
LPTB	London Passenger Transport Board
LSWR	London and South Western Railway
LRT	London Regional Transport
LTB	London Transport Board
LTE	London Transport Executive
MDR	Metropolitan District Railway
MET.R	Metropolitan Railway
MET. & GC Jt	Metropolitan and Great Central Joint
MID.R	Midland Railway
WLR	West London Railway (GW & LNW)
WLER	West London Extension Railway (GW, LBSC, LNW & LSWR)

Undertakings in bold lettering in the main took over from the original companies. For the main lines there were two stages — take over by the 'Big Four' in 1923 and then by British Railways in 1948. For the underground railways there was one principal stage, the take over by the LPTB in 1933. (This was succeeded in turn by LTE, LTB, LTE and LRT.)

11 Kenton LNWR/LMSR/BR(LMR) G* P
c.1923/3 November *1985 TQ 169881*

London's first main line railway, the London and Birmingham, was opened between Euston and Boxmoor in the Chilterns in 1837. The growth of traffic was reflected by the augmentation of the original double track by a third track in 1859, and

Kenton line 1923

a fourth in 1875. These carried main line traffic, but by 1911 the LNW followed the underground lines and the Great Western in realising the potential of Middlesex for suburban development. Rather than compete with the underground lines, the LNW became associated with them. In 1912 a new double track railway was opened alongside the existing railway as far out as Bushey, where it diverged on a new route to Watford. Although it was planned for electric trains, under wartime conditions the completion of the Stonebridge Park power station was delayed until 1916, and it was not until 1917 that electric trains running from the Bakerloo line, replaced steam. Initially, these were drawn from existing lines, but from 1920 special stock, owned jointly by the LNW and the London Electric Railway, was introduced. In 1922 this was joined by full size trains of the LNW, shortly to become part of the LMS. A number of stations were opened on the new line in 1912, one of which was Kenton.

The two photographs are taken from a footbridge to the south of Kenton Station. (The separation of the tracks is arranged to avoid the supports of the bridge.) The low angle of the sides of the cutting indicates the somewhat unstable clay subsoil. At this point the width had to be sufficient not only to accommodate the new line and the station platforms, but also a goods yard

Kenton line 1985

opened in 1911, which was reached by the original lines. Signalling remained manual on the electric lines until 1932, and three signal posts appear in the view of 1923. Tallest is the post with two co-acting arms with rings attached, controlling the down slow line. An electric train has just left the down platform but the station's down home has already been put back to the 'on' position. The shortest of the posts is in the 'off' position, giving another tube train a clear run towards Wembley. This consists of Joint LNWR/ LER stock, working through to Elephant and Castle on the Bakerloo line. There is no goods shed, as the yard only handled coal class, mineral and station to station traffic in truck loads. Most of the open wagons would be loaded with

domestic coal for the houses built in the fields around the station. (Houses under construction on the Churchill Estate can be seen at the left of the view.) The loading gauge at the entrance to the yard belongs to a period when flat or open wagons could be loaded to different heights.

The goods yard was closed in 1965, and most of the site, viewed in 1985, has been sold by the railway. The semaphore signals have gone, and since 1966, the steam lines have been electrified on the 25 KV overhead wire system. This is far more visually obtrusive than the live rails. The gantries obscure the parts of the view that have changed least — namely, the tracks electrified with live rails and the station of 1912. Elsewhere in London, main routes have been electrified, but the former LNW is the only one to have overhead wires and live rails following the same route.

12 Stanmore LNWR/LMSR/BR(LMR) GPHC
12 April 1952/3 November 1985 TQ 168919

The 1952 view shows the station building at the terminus of the two mile branch line, from Harrow and Wealdstone on the LNW main line to Stanmore. This was promoted by Mr Gordon, owner of the Gordon Hotel chain, who provided ninety per cent of the original capital. His interest in the district was initially concentrated on Bentley Priory, which he bought and converted into an hotel. In order to obtain the co-operation of the parish council, he provided an elaborate terminal building. Few engineering works were needed for the line, which probably facilitated the expenditure on the station. From 1890, when it was opened, the line was served by LNW trains, and in 1899 the LNW absorbed the Harrow and Stanmore Company. In 1932, a halt was opened at Belmont, at the same time as a competing line

was opened to Stanmore by the Metropolitan Railway. This provided through rush hour trains to Baker Street and the City, but fortunately for the branch, the decline in traffic from its terminus was offset by growth at Belmont. The existence of the rival station was formally recognised in 1950, when Stanmore was renamed 'Stanmore Village', and recognised in a less welcome way in 1952, when it was closed to passengers. The branch remained open for goods traffic and carried passengers as far as Belmont until 1964.

The buttressed porch, with its threshold illuminated by two gas lamps, made an impressive entrance to the station building. Resting on the porch was a clock in a fine case of stone. The porch adjoined a low tower with battlements, creating a military effect, and a spirelet provided an ecclesiastical touch. This spirelet was made of oak, sheeted with lead. The offices were arranged to the right of the tower, under a gabled roof, and had two three-light,

Stanmore 1952

Stanmore 1985

Tudor-style windows. There was a gargoyle at each corner of the tower. The station was built of red brick with stone dressings, and a pitched tiled roof. In accordance with country custom, a letterbox was built into the front wall.

Soon after closure to passengers, two out of the four gargoyles were removed, together with the porch and clock. The lamp posts followed, and despite boarding up of doors and windows to prevent entry, roof tiles began to disappear. The site was purchased for housing development in 1969, and in 1970 the letterbox, still marked 'LMS Station', was removed. After protracted negotiations with the planners, rather than demolish the station building, it was agreed that it would be virtually rebuilt. Examination of the two views will show the way in which the top half of the tower and spirelet, together with the ornate chimneys, were removed. The roof was retiled, and three dormer windows were inserted. New facing bricks were used, but the stone surrounds

for the windows and the quatrefoil were all replaced. There are not many station buildings in the London area that have been made into dwellings, but Stanmore provides a good example of such a reconstruction.

13 Southall Station GWR/BR(WR) GPFLHC
6 June 1959/29 March 1986 TQ 128799

The Great Western main line was opened from its first terminus at Paddington to a point short of Maidenhead Bridge in 1838. It was essentially a main line and little attempt was made to foster local traffic. However, a station was opened at Southall in 1839. With the opening of the Brentford branch in 1859, this became a junction and also acquired an engine shed. Two standard gauge tracks were added on the up side of the broad gauge tracks, reaching out from Paddington as far as Southall in 1877. The growth of traffic was reflected in the construction

Southall 1959

of new station buildings in a characteristic Great Western style in 1876. After the Second World War, Southall continued to grow, and the railway passenger traffic increased, although some freight passed to road transport, and Southall was closed to goods in 1967.

The first photograph of 1959 shows a typical outer suburban train of the period. The locomotive, No.6167, belongs to the 61XX class, designed by C.B. Collett for London suburban services. No.6167 was built by the GW at Swindon works in 1935 and withdrawn in 1965. Being built for passenger work, it incorporated such GW features as a brass safety valve cover, and a copper cap for the chimney. Its six coach train includes compartment stock from both GW and BR. Its appearance was sufficient to arouse the interest of the three young train spotters on the opposite platform. Not only the train, but the whole scene shows little change from the 1930s,

with gas lamps and water cranes. The starting signal is a colour light, but there is a wooden semaphore arm on the centre platform. ATC ramps are visible in both the down main and down relief tracks. The space between the main line tracks indicates that the lines were laid to the broad gauge until 1892.

Comparison between 1959 and 1986 may begin with the train: steam-hauled coaches have been replaced by three-coach multiple unit set No. L410. The engines were built by Leyland, and the coach bodies were by Pressed Steel. Coincidentally, these units were introduced in 1959, the same year as that of the first photograph. Southall East SB was closed in 1968, and the only signal in the 1986 view is on the site of the up starter. Not only have the gas lamps and the water cranes gone, but also a considerable part of the station buildings. The platform canopy has been removed from the platform on the extreme left and partly removed from the centre platform. The station buildings over the relief lines have

Southall 1986

been demolished. The building on the extreme left is not directly associated with the station, having been built in the early twentieth century for a margarine manufacturing company. However, it is now used by a railway preservation group who have already acquired eight locomotives.

14 Colnbrook GWR/BR(WR) GPFLHC
25 September 1956/29 March 1986 TQ 036766

The town of Staines was served by the LSW from 1848, but this did not prevent the opening of a competing line, branching from the Great Western at West Drayton. This reached Colnbrook in 1884, and Staines in 1885. Passenger traffic from Staines was never very great, but Colnbrook's contribution was supplemented by four halts (Colnbrook Estate Halt was not opened until 1961). Freight developed, with a number of private sidings,

including the Shell Mex and BP depot, opened at Staines in 1964. Unfortunately for the GW branch, by restoring a short wartime spur at Yeoveney, it proved possible to serve this from the LSW line. The passenger service on the GW Staines branch was withdrawn in 1965; after the cessation of public goods traffic in 1966, the branch relied solely on private siding traffic. When the Staines oil terminal was transferred to the LSW line, there was nothing left south of Colnbrook. In 1974, Colnbrook appeared to have a certain future as an oil fuel terminal for Heathrow Airport, but this traffic seems to have been lost to a pipeline.

When the first photograph was taken in 1956, traffic was still quite heavy. The picture was taken from the signal box, which operated both the passing place in the station and also the adjoining level crossing. Equipment for giving up and for receiving the tablets, which gave authority for working over the two single line sections on either side of Colnbrook, may be seen on both sides of the line.

The arm of the down starting signal is fixed to a standard post, and is positioned well down it to

Colnbrook 1956

Colnbrook 1986

avoid the station canopy obstructing its sightline. No footbridge was provided, so passengers from up-trains used a foot crossing made of old sleepers. However, the person using it in the picture is not a passenger but Mrs Lawrence, who acted as ticket collector and porter at Colnbrook in 1956. The station building with its gabled end is the original building of 1884, with the goods shed in the background. The service was being maintained by a push-pull set and a diesel railcar. On this occasion the diesel railcar was running from West Drayton to Staines — that is, towards the camera — and the push-pull set was going in the opposite direction. Diesel railcar No. W27W was built with an AEC chassis and a Park Royal body for the GW in 1940, and operated until 1960. 0-4-2T locomotive No. 1436 was built by Swindon works in 1934 as No. 4836. C.B. Collett based the design on a well-tried class from the 1880s. No. 1436 remained in service until 1950.

A few features appear in both the 1956 and

1986 views. Most conspicuous is the telegraph pole, but the small building beyond the iron railings, with the vent at the side, can also be seen in both. While the down-platform has survived, all the buildings have been replaced. The prominent lamp-posts and the pipes on the left hand side of the tracks were provided for the oil terminal, constructed on the site of the up platform. At the moment, the prospects of Colnbrook as a railhead seem uncertain.

15 West Hampstead Mid.R/LMSR/BR(LMR)
17 October 1925/29 October 1955/24 July 1986 TQ 258848

In its early days, traffic from the Midland Railway reached London over the LNWR line to Euston. From 1858 it used a new line from Leicester via Bedford to Hitchin and the Great Northern main line to Kings Cross. Increasing traffic spurred the Midland directors to promote their own extension from Bedford to London, and this was opened to passenger traffic in 1868. Before this, in 1860 the Hampstead Junction Railway had been completed between Camden and Willesden, and the Midland's London extension passed under the HJR to reach the western portal of Belsize Park tunnel. The bridge not only carried trains on the HJR, but also had a footpath for pedestrians, which provided a 'grand stand' view of trains on the Midland Railway. The three views that follow were taken in 1925, 1955, and 1986 from this bridge.

When the first photograph was taken, the chimneys of the electric power station were still visible on the left. At this point there were six running lines, those nearest the power station carrying local trains, the centre pair for express trains, and those in the foreground carrying goods traffic. A typical Midland signal post in the centre bears the down starter arm for Finchley Road Signal Box: below it is the West Hampstead

West Hampstead 1925

distant signal. The insulators near the finial hold the wires conveying electric current to the signal box to indicate that the oil lamps are burning. The white diamond, visible between the arms, informed locomotive crews of trains stopped at the signal that, as an electric track circuit warned the signalman of the position of the train, they were not required to report their presence to the signal box. The down express train is being hauled by locomotive No. 1047, built by the LMS at Derby in 1924, and withdrawn by BR in 1954. Although built after the formation of the LMS, at the beginning of 1923, it was a typical Midland compound locomotive.

The 1955 view shows virtually no change in the arrangement of the tracks, although the up main line has been relaid with flat-bottomed track. However, much of the electric power station has been demolished, and the adjacent sidings, which held freight wagons in 1925, are in use for stabling passenger coaches. The sidings on the

West Hampstead 1955

West Hampstead 1986

right survive and these is a new depot for the chocolate manufacturers, Cadbury. The Midland's wooden signal posts have all been replaced by LMS steel posts, with upper quadrant arms. A freight train, hauled by an LMS 0-6-0 tank locomotive, a 'Jinty', is being held on the down goods line. A Jubilee class locomotive, No.45694, 'Bellerophon', is approaching on a down express. This was built to the design of Sir William Stanier at Crewe in 1936 and was withdrawn by BR in 1967.

The 1925 photograph, although taken in early LMS days, shows a Midland view, that of 1955 taken in BR days shows an LMS view, while that of 1986 marks the great change after electrification between St. Pancras and Bedford. The site of the power station has been occupied by new buildings and the sidings have gone. The decline in goods traffic is reflected in the removal of the sidings and also in the reduction from six to five running lines. The Finchley Road signal box and its semaphore signals have been removed, but none of the colour lights which replaced them are visible. The masts and wires of the 25 KV overhead electrification are a prominent feature. The train consists of a four-coach multiple unit electric set forming the 14.50 from St. Pancras to

Bedford. It is of the BR 317 class, built in York in 1981 for the St. Pancras electrification, except for the intermediate trailers, which were built at Derby. Visible in the background on the right is the entrance to the original Belsize Tunnel of 1868 which carried interlaced tracks until the opening of the parallel Belsize New Tunnel in 1884.

16 Ealing Broadway MDR/LPTB/LTE/LTB/ LRT P*
18 February 1956/28 April 1986 TQ 180809

London's first underground railway, the Metropolitan, described a semi-circle to the north of central London. To complete the southern half of the circle, a separate company, the Metropolitan District, was formed, and the first section of its covered way, between South Kensington and Westminster, was opened in 1868. To channel more pasengers on to this very expensive section, extensions were made into the more prosperous western suburbs, either by new construction or running powers over the tracks of main line companies. For instance in 1877, by means of running powers over the LSW, District line trains reached Richmond. A new line, leaving the LSW at Turnham Green, brought the Metropolitan District to a terminal at Ealing adjoining the Great Western main line. Between 1883 and 1885 District trains ran through to Windsor, but their austere rolling stock proved unpopular for runs of this length. In contrast, the through service between Ealing Broadway and Southend, which lasted from 1910 until 1939, used main line rolling stock.

The terminus at Ealing was initially a two-track station with an overall roof. A third track was added on the outer face of the southern platform. For many years it was operated independently, but as part of a rebuilding plan in 1966 booking and other facilities were combined

Ealing Broadway 1956

with those of the Central line of LT and the Western Region of BR.

The first view was taken in 1956 from the eastern end of the northern platform. Steam traction ceased in 1905, but a water tower, bereft of its iron tank, appears on the left hand side of the view. The pump house was reached through the round-headed door in the end of the building, and this was used for storage after the demise of steam traction reduced the demand for water. Electro-pneumatic signalling was introduced at the same time as electrification, the points and signals being operated from the signal box on the right hand side. The windows were bricked up during the Second World War. After the War, a new box opened at the top of the bank on the left of the picture, working with colour lights and power-operated points. The approaching train consists of a mix of clerestory-roofed coaches, built in the late twenties and early thirties, and stock built before and after the Second World War with a characteristic outward flare at the base of its side.

The most striking feature of the 1986 view is

Ealing Broadway 1986

the survival of the water tower. Other continuing features are the bridge carrying cables, the railings and the shed which adjoined the site of the demolished signal box. Although the signals are no longer operated from the 'new' box, both the running signal, WP 55 and the ground signal WP 51 remain unchanged, only the direction indicator under WP 55 having been replaced. Sidings have been removed but rails are still supported in chairs, the special needs of London Transport being better served by this type than the flat-bottom track adopted by BR. Differences in detail include the new lamp, but more striking is the large mirror, provided for the use of drivers of one-man-operated trains. The train consists of the new unpainted 1980s stock, a contrast to the familiar red of the 1956 train. Because developments came earlier on the underground lines, the two views show less fundamental change than might be found on BR.

17 Alperton Station MDR/LPTB/LTE/LTB/ LRT P*
c.1910/25 July 1981 TQ 181838

Most of the extensions of the Metropolitan District, thrust out to collect traffic from the west, joined exisiting main lines, as at Wimbledon and Ealing. However, two extensions, both promoted by nominally independent companies, penetrated green field sites in anticipation of development. Both branched out from the extension to Ealing, the first reaching Hounslow in 1883 and the second being opened to South Harrow in 1903. In character, they fell between the conventional speculative line, such as the Bexley Heath Railway of 1895, and the underground railway to which they were connected. They were surface railways, with

Alperton Station 1910

Alperton Station 1981

engineering works similar to other lines, but they had no facilities for freight traffic. The great advantage they offered to passengers was their ability to convey them to a choice of stations in the City and West End.

The Metropolitan District unsuccessfully sought powers to extend across the fields between Ealing and Uxbridge in 1879. The nominally independent Ealing and South Harrow line was authorised in 1894, and an extension to Uxbridge, associated with landowners, obtained its Act in 1897. In the event, the Harrow and Uxbridge was transferred to the Metropolitan Railway. Construction of the Ealing and South Harrow was complete by 1899, but it was not opened until 1903. The delay reflected the financial difficulties encountered by the Metropolitan District, which ended with the takeover by American interests. One of the objectives of the Metropolitan District was electrification, and the Ealing and South Harrow was duly electrified, with a temporary power station at Alperton, and used for training purposes. An electric train depot was constructed at South Harrow, and when the line was finally opened in 1903, it was the first section of the District system to be operated with electric traction. (Travellers to the West End and City changed into steam trains at Mill Hill Park — now Acton Town — until 1905.)

All the stations were opened in 1903, and since that time, none have been closed and no new stations have been added. This reflects the way in which development took place after the stations had been opened. Alperton was a hamlet, about one mile (1½km) south of Wembley, where there was a station on the LNW main line. The Grand Junction Canal passed Alperton, but apart from the occasional Sunday school outing, did not carry passenger traffic. London was left behind at Ealing and apart from the great show ground at Park Royal, the line traversed farm land until it reached Alperton. William Course, who at the age of 54 had already served the District for over 30 years, was transferred from Sloane Square to take charge of the new stations at Park Royal, Alperton and Sudbury Town. A house was provided for him at the foot of the embankment on the south side of the station. (This was demolished in the 1930s to make way for a new bus garage.) In the first photograph, taken about 1910, the front of the station house is visible under the bridge. The station offices were built on the north side, with timber framing and corrugated iron. There was a subway under the line, and the platforms were reached by long flights of steps, protected by canopies — the tops are visible in the photograph. The name Alperton Station was displayed on the bridge, although until 1910, because of the comparative insignificance of Alperton, the station was named 'Perivale — Alperton'. The electro-pneumatic signal, for the eastbound trains, appears to the right of the bridge. At road level, a gas lamp, telegraph poles and a horse and cart are visible, and the taking of a photograph in Alperton was enough of an event to cause all those in view to stand and stare.

Terraced housing began to cover the fields between the station and Wembley before the First World War, but the great period of development took place between the wars, when terrace blocks and semi-detached houses filled the gap between Ealing and Alperton. From 1910, some of the trains had been extended to Uxbridge. In 1932 the District trains were replaced by tube trains operating from the Piccadilly line. The mushroom growth of traffic was catered for with new buildings, and the one built at Alperton in 1933 apears in the 1981 view. The essential design, with booking hall at ground level, and steps up to the platforms remained unchanged, but well designed brick, concrete and glass construction replaced timber and iron. An escalator was added in 1955 for the eastbound platform. By 1981, the station name has been moved from a new bridge to the building, with the 'Underground' sign transferred to a retaining wall. Integration with bus services is illustrated by the use of the station forecourt as a terminal for route 79 to Burnt Oak Broadway. The rear platform bus, stopped outside the station, was operating on route 83, between Golders Green and Slough. The electro-pneumatic signal on the railway has been replaced by a colour light, and the gas lamps in the road by electricity. Shops, traffic lights and a bus stop sign are all significant additions. Between 1910 and 1981, Alperton had seen more change than was usual.

18 Rayners Lane Station Met.Rly/LPTB/LTE/ LTB/LRT G* P*
August 1922/20 July 1957 TQ 128 875

The impetus for the construction of the Harrow and Uxbridge Railway came from local land-owners, anxious for an alternative to the long-established GW branch to Uxbridge, in association with Underground railway companies. Initially, it was intended as an extension of the Ealing and South Harrow line which was associated with the Metropolitan District company. However, partly because of the financial problems from which the District Railway was suffering at the time, a new arrangement was made with the Metropolitan Railway including a junction at Harrow-on-the-Hill. The connection to the Ealing and South Harrow was constructed, but was used only to

Rayners Lane 1922

Rayners Lane 1957

reach a gasworks until it began to carry a passenger service in 1910. The junction between the line to South Harrow and the connection to the Metropolitan was just to the east of the overbridge carrying Rayners Lane. The Harrow and Uxbridge ran through similar country to the Ealing and South Harrow, described as 'open, sparsely inhabited country composed of elm-lined lanes and hayfields'. However, unlike the E & SH on which all the stations were opened at the same time as the line, the H & U had only one intermediate station, at Ruislip. Electrification work was not complete, so the line was operated by steam trains from 1904 until the beginning of 1905. Again, unlike the E & SH, most of the stations either had complete facilities for freight traffic, or at least handled coal and full wagon traffic until 1964, when goods trains ceased to run.

Additional halts were provided at Ickenham, opened in 1905, followed by Eastcote and Rayners Lane in 1906. (Ruislip Manor followed in 1912, and finally, West Harrow in 1913.) The first photograph shows Rayners Lane in 1922. The booking office was up on the road, and serpentine paths ran obliquely down to the wooden platforms on either side of the line. The simplicity of the waiting shelter, visible on the up platform, contrasts with the provision of electric lighting. A station name board adjoins the shelter, with the background of the Metropolitan's red diamond adopted in 1915. The lines to Harrow-on-the-Hill (Metropolitan) and South Harrow (District) diverge just beyond the bridge, and the junction signal box stands in the fork. This was a mechanical box which worked the points and signals by rodding and wires. The lower quadrant junction signal, set for the District line, may be seen, and also the ground signal for the crossover.

From 1929 housing development was rapid, some of it associated with the railway's subsidiary company, Metropolitan Railway Country Estates Ltd. London Transport rebuilt the station in 1938, in the progressive style adopted for all their new station buildings. A large booking hall at

road level spanned the tracks, with steps leading down to the platform. Concrete replaced wood for platforms and fences. The tube train in the 1957 view, consisting of stock built for the Bakerloo line in 1938, has come from the Piccadilly line. Some of the trains ran through to Uxbridge while others used a reversing siding at Rayners Lane. The goods yard, opened in 1929 to serve new housing development, was behind the fence on the right hand side. It was closed in 1967. The two views reflect the transformation of what was once rural Middlesex.

19 Sudbury GCR/LNER/BR(LMR) GPFHC
1958/3 November 1985 TQ 152858

In 1906 the Great Central Railway published a poster headed 'Live in the Country', announcing their new series of suburban trains to serve the 'picturesque district' beyond Harrow. This marked the completion of lines giving the GC access to London. The GC had first reached the new terminus at Marylebone over Metropolitan Railway tracks in 1899. An elaborate agreement of 1906 transferred the Metropolitan line from Harrow-on-the-Hill to Verney Junction to a Metropolitan and Great Central Joint Committee. An alternative route was provided by the new Great Western and Great Central Joint line via High Wycombe, rejoining the original route at Grendon Underwood Junction. To reach this a line was constructed by the GC from Neasden Junction on the Metropolitan route, to Northolt Junction on the GW and GC. It was only 6¼ miles (10 km) in length, but was an expensive line, partly because of the difficulty of crossing established railways and also on account of the heavy clay subsoil. Although it was built as a connecting line for express services, three local stations were opened in 1906 at Wembley Hill, Sudbury and Harrow Road and South Harrow

and Roxeth (later Sudbury Hill), all with side platforms on loop lines to avoid interference with express trains. In addition to passengers, the three stations handled all types of goods traffic.

The two pictures were taken from a footbridge to the west of Sudbury and Harrow Road Station. At this point the line climbs at 1 in 264 into the cutting, the gentle slopes of which reflect the instability of the clay subsoil. This in itself necessitated the purchase of more land, while the provision of a third track, forming a siding, led to even greater expense. For the station, separate through and platform lines were provided. The approaching train is about to take the up platform loop, as indicated by the upper quadrant arm of the junction signal. In the foreground, a GC signal with lower quadrant arm and wooden post is lowered for the passage of a train from the down-platform loop. The upper quadrant signal with the concrete post applied to the down main line, and was erected by the LNE. The ground signal,

Sudbury 1958

Sudbury 1985

Wood Lane Station 1920

Wood Lane Station 1963

elevated on the GC post in the foreground, controlled access to the down-siding. The two coaches of LNE vintage are being pulled by an 0-6-2 tank locomotive of the N7 class, first built for the GE, but perpetuated by LNE construction between 1924 and 1928. Withdrawal of the N7 class took place from 1958 until 1962. Perhaps the most surprising feature of the 1958 photograph is the short length of the train in an area which, particularly in the period of the 1930s, experienced major growth. Unfortunately, both South Harrow (later Sudbury Hill) and Sudbury and Harrow Road Stations were within a stone's throw of LT stations which, with their frequent electric services, have attracted most of the traffic.

The second photograph shows the removal of all the signals and all the tracks, except for the two main running lines, which have been re-located to serve the platforms. The facilities for handling goods traffic were withdrawn in 1965, and the only passenger service now runs on to the former GW and GC line, terminating at High Wycombe, Princes Risborough or Banbury. With an alternative station so near, few trains now stop at Sudbury and Harrow and the platform has a neglected air. However, the photograph shows the way in which a view of 1985 still conveys something of the scale of enterprise undertaken during the high summer of the railways.

20 Wood Lane Station CLR/LPTB P*
September 1920/8 June 1963 TQ 234803

The Central London was the third electric tube railway to be constructed in London. An act of Parliament was obtained in 1891 and the line was opened under one of London's main traffic arteries, between the Bank and Shepherd's Bush in 1900. There were no class distinctions on its trains, and because of its standard fare, the Central London became known as the

'Twopenny Tube'. The line was carried between Bank and Shepherd's Bush in two tubes, but at the western end, an extension in a single tube led to the generating station and car depot, above the ground. The opening of the White City exhibition centre provided the incentive to construct a station beyond the depot. To avoid the reversal of trains, a second tube line was provided between Shepherd's Bush and the new station, forming a loop which trains followed in an anti-clockwise direction. To handle large crowds visiting the White City, platforms at ground level were provided on both sides of the single line.

The western end of this station of 1908, named Wood Lane, is shown in the photograph of September 1920. The Central London Railway became part of the underground group from the beginning of 1913, and this is reflected by the station name boards with the name backed by a solid red disc in the underground style. To facilitate passenger movement, and also because of the frequency of the train service, station furniture such as seats was sparse on tube platforms, and all that is visible is a penny-in-the-slot weighing machine and one seat. In fact, the platforms illustrated lost much of their traffic during the month before the photograph was taken, when the Central London trains were extended over the Great Western-owned Ealing and Shepherd's Bush Railway. New lines descended from each side of the loop to sub-surface platforms for the use of trains to Ealing, giving Wood Lane four platform faces and three platform lines.

The layout changed radically in 1947 when this complicated arrangement was replaced by a new station, opened on the surface in the Ealing direction, and named 'White City'. The Wood Lane platforms were closed to passengers, and new access lines were built to the car depot. The second photograph, taken in 1963, shows the western end of the 1908 station, after the removal of track and some years of disuse. It represents the very considerable contribution to the revenue of London Underground railways provided by exhibition centres.

THREE

North and East of London

The railway system to the east of London differs appreciably from that of the west. To begin with, the Dockland area, at least until the 1960s, was a major point of origin and destination for freight traffic. Commuting traffic developed sooner and included a far higher proportion of passengers using workmen's tickets, rather than season tickets. The principal company in east London, the Great Eastern, had more in common with the South Eastern than the companies that served the Midlands and the North. It carried some coal traffic, originating on the GE and GN joint line in the Doncaster area, but a vital proportion of its revenue came from passenger traffic in the London area. It constructed suburban railways to places like Enfield, Chingford and Loughton and commuters poured into its London terminals at Liverpool Street and Fenchurch Street on a scale unknown to Paddington or Euston.

There was development between the wars, but it was not on the scale of the 'flooding' of Middlesex, and there was certainly no equivalent of 'Metroland' in Essex. Whereas the underground companies projected their services over new lines into Middlesex, the first penetration to the east involved running over an existing line to Barking. The only new underground line of the inter-war period in this area, the extension of the Piccadilly line to Cockfosters, sought traffic to the north rather than east. The LNE as successor to the GE and the LMS to the LTS, considered electrification but instead developed steam services. (The LNE executed the first peace time closure when services from Fenchurch Street to Blackwall and North Greenwich were withdrawn in 1926.) Following the establishment of the

London Passenger Transport Board, an arrangement for pooling passenger revenue was accompanied by plans for underground trains to run over former GN lines to the north and over GE lines to the north east of London. After wartime delay, trains from the LT Central line reached Stratford in 1946, and, in stages, completed the Hainault loop by 1948 and reached Ongar in 1949. The new route was in tube tunnels in the inner area and over former steam operated lines further out. Passenger services to Beckton, with its gasworks, and to Gallions, for the docks, ended in 1940 and those over the North London line to Poplar in 1944. To the north, the service to Palace Gates finished in 1963. However, the early sixties was the period when many of the former GE lines, together with the LTS, were finally electrified. Less foreseeable developments came later, in the inner area. Firstly, in 1985, the well-established service from Richmond to Broad Street was diverted to North Woolwich, with electrification and the opening of some new stations between Dalston and North Woolwich. Even more surprisingly, the GE from Fenchurch Street to Blackwall and to Greenwich, together with the NL between Poplar and Bow with an extension to Stratford, were scheduled for re-opening as the Docklands Light Railway in 1987. In the 1940s the railways of east London were the least developed in the metropolis; in the 1980s they have at least caught up.

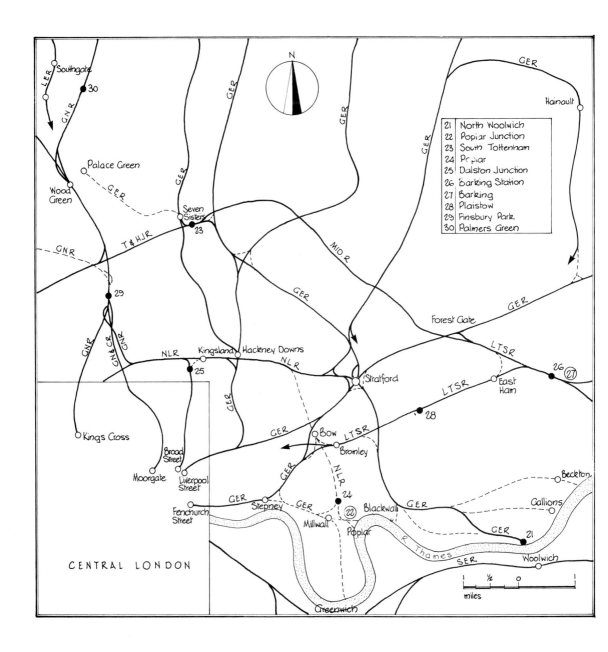

21	North Woolwich
22	Poplar Junction
23	South Tottenham
24	Poplar
25	Dalston Junction
26	Barking Station
27	Barking
28	Plaistow
29	Finsbury Park
30	Palmers Green

CENTRAL LONDON

Abbreviations

BR(ER)	British Railways (Eastern Region)
BR(LMR)	British Railways (London, Midland Region)
GER	Great Eastern Railway
GNR	Great Northern Railway
GN & CR	Great Northern and City Railway
LER	London Electric Railway
LMSR	London Midland and Scottish Railway
LNER	London and North Eastern Railway
LTSR	London, Tilbury and Southend Railway
Mid.R.	Midland Railway
NLR	North London Railway
SER	South Eastern Railway
T & HJR	Tottenham and Hampstead Junction Railway (GE and MID)

Undertakings in bold lettering, in the main took over from the original companies. For the main lines there were two stages — 'take over' by the 'Big Four' in 1923, followed by British Railways in 1948. For the underground railways, there was one principal stage — 'take over' by the LPTB in 1933. (This was succeeded in turn by LTE, LTB, LTE and LRT.)

21 North Woolwich GER/LNER/BR(ER) GPFLH
21 January 1956/12 November 1977/10 August 1979/27 March 1986 TQ 432798

Stratford Station was opened on the Eastern Counties Railway between Mile End and Romford in 1939. In order to reach the River Thames, the Stratford and Thames Junction Railway was authorised to a wharf near the mouth of Bow Creek in 1845. An act was obtained for an extension following the river through un-inhabited country to a point opposite the south bank town of Woolwich, with its important arsenal, in the same Parliamentary session. The line was completed to a remote point on the north bank in 1847 and was operated by the Eastern Counties Railway. The station was named North Woolwich and, with a connecting ferry across the Thames, it provided the only railway route to Woolwich until the opening of the North Kent line of the South Eastern in 1849. A pier was constructed during the years 1848 and 1849, and the railway ferry operated until 1908. This was remarkable, as the London County Council had provided a free ferry from 1889 — presumably the railway ferry was used by holders of through-tickets to Woolwich. Faced with the competition of the direct SE route, the EC promoted riverside pleasure gardens, and also reconstructed the station buildings in 1854. However, the future of the line depended on neither traffic to Woolwich nor visitors to the pleasure gardens, but rather on the major developments of docks and industry, which incidentally necessitated a diversion of a section of the line. Between the wars, the construction of Silvertown Way and the provision of a trolley bus service eroded passenger traffic. Particularly from the 1960s, the decline of the dock system led to the loss of most of the freight traffic. By 1969, passenger trains were using only one track between Custom House and North Woolwich, and closure seemed imminent.

The first photograph, although taken in 1956, shows North Woolwich much as it would have appeared after its last major reconstruction in 1890. The fine station building, through which passengers would have passed to the ferry or the pleasure gardens, is seen on the right. Between the side platform and an island platform there are three tracks, the centre of which is an engine release road. During the period when North Woolwich had an intensive service, the engine from a terminating train would have stopped by the pit, short of the ground signal. If a driver started inadvertently before being cleared by the ground signal, his locomotive would have struck the scotch block, visible in front of the timber crossing. While waiting to take out the next train,

North Woolwich 1956

North Woolwich 1977

North Woolwich 1979

North Woolwich 1986

locomotive firemen would have cleared the fire-box and the smokebox, the débris contributing to the pile of ashes visible in the picture. The line of white standards were gassing points as the North Woolwich line had the distinction of being served by gas-lit coaches until after the Second World War. Platform lighting, however, was by standard LNE electric lamps. In 1858, a spur was constructed to the new LTS line, and by running over it, trains from North Woolwich reached Fenchurch Street instead of the EC terminus at Shoreditch. This spur remained in use until 1940, when trains ran to Stratford (Low Level) with peak hour extensions to Palace Gates or Tottenham Hale. The train in the photograph was the 14.51 bound for Stratford, departing on a Saturday afternoon in winter. It consisted of an N7 class locomotive and an LNE five-coach articulated set.

The second photograph, taken in 1977, shows North Woolwich at its nadir. The goods yard was closed in 1970, leaving only one track serving one side of the island platform. In 1977, the basic service of two trains per hour, with peak period extensions to Tottenham Hale was maintained by two coach diesel sets, so no engine release facilities were required. The Southern Region train from which the view was taken was a rail tour special to North Woolwich consisting of two four-car TC sets and a buffet car with traction provided by a class 33 diesel electric locomotive No.33103. With the advent of the Greater London Council, a policy of reviving public transport was formulated, and in 1979 this affected North Woolwich. The side platform was restored, and a new booking office was erected on the south side of the original station building. An improved train service was part of the plan to revive the dockland area. For a while the fate of the old building was undetermined, but in 1985 it was re-opened as a railway museum, specialising in the history of the Great Eastern Railway. The fourth photograph, taken in 1986, shows the building so well renovated that in 1985, it won an award as the best restored railway station in Britain. The original lamp posts carry new lamps, and the platform has been resurfaced. However, from the point of view of train services, the most significant change is the addition of the live rail. In 1985, the line was electrified and the Richmond to Broad Street service was diverted to North Woolwich. An off-peak service of three electric trains per hour should do much to restore passenger traffic on the North Woolwich line, even if the heavy freight traffic has gone beyond recall.

22 Poplar Junction GER/LNER/BR(ER)
11 November 1954/27 March 1986/27 March 1986 TQ 383806

The London and Blackwall Railway was opened in 1840 as a passenger-only line, partly to serve the East End and the docks, but also to serve the paddle steamers operating from Blackwall to Woolwich and Gravesend. Originally operated by cable, it was converted to locomotive traction from 1849. Passenger traffic declined and in 1926, the eastern end was closed to passengers. However, the section between Fenchurch Street and Stepney has remained in use, and in 1987 the route as far as Millwall Junction is due to re-open as part of the Docklands Light Railway.

Because barges had the right to enter or leave the docks without payment, goods could be conveyed from ships to riverside wharves without payment for transport to the dock companies. To exploit this, all the principal railway companies opened docks or wharves on the Thames. The Midland Railway reached London in 1868, and the Tottenham and Hampstead Railway gave access to the Great Eastern system. By a somewhat tortuous route, via Tottenham and Stratford, the Midland was able to reach a dock which it opened in Poplar in 1882. A branch, leaving the London and Blackwall line between Millwall Junction and Poplar, ran for a quarter of

a mile to the water's edge, where a stop signal was provided, predictably in a fixed position.

The first view was taken at Poplar Junction, on the former London and Blackwall Railway looking east in 1954. Passenger traffic ceased in 1926, and freight was negligible from 1961, although closure was delayed until 1966. In the same way, the Midland's Poplar Dock, served by the diverging tracks, was officially closed in 1956, although there had been no traffic for some years. The two overbridges carried Blackwall Way, and the platforms of the Great Eastern's Poplar Station are visible under the bridge on the left. A number of features contribute to an impression of the Midland Railway Company. The workshops in the fork and the hydraulic power station on the right, have the characteristic red and blue brickwork of the Midland, and the iron glazing frames in the windows of the workshop are unmistakeable. Unfortunately, the best feature of all, a vintage Midland signal box is concealed by the pier supporting the middle of the road-bridge. This was provided with Midland and LMS signals, examples of both appearing in front of the workshops. The dock was badly damaged during the war and traffic was almost non-existent, but because the branch was still open in 1954, the signal box was preserved and occasionally manned.

Two views show the transformation in 1986. The link between the photographs is the tower of the hydraulic power station, on the right hand

Poplar Junction 1954

Poplar Junction 1986

Poplar Junction 1986

side in each of the three views. The metal parapet of the bridge over the Blackwall line and the brick of that over the Midland also provide a link. Poplar Junction was below ground level, and by 1986 the site was buried in tipped material. The site of the dock had been occupied by Messrs Charringtons. Apart from the remains of the hydraulic power station, there is little left to mark a site once busy with railway traffic.

23 South Tottenham Station GER & Mid.R./ LNER & LMSR/BR(ER) P
*17 December **1955**/25 March **1986** TQ 337887*

At a time when the M25 motorway is about to complete its circuit of London, it may be noted that the corresponding rail circuit, although made up of various sections, was almost completed in the 1860s. One section was opened by the Tottenham and Hampstead Junction company in 1868, describing an arc between the radial lines of the Midland from St. Pancras and the GE route along the Lea valley from Stratford. Trains were operated by the Midland and GE companies and in 1902 the T & HJ was replaced by a Midland and GE joint committee, duly transformed to an LMS and LNE joint committee in 1923. South Tottenham Station was opened in 1871, and in time became an extremely busy junction. First, in 1879 a spur was opened at the west end of the station, leading to Seven Sisters on the line to Enfield. This was followed by the Tottenham and Forest Gate line of 1894, branching off at the east end. Although the station did not handle a great number of passengers, the number of trains calling or passing through was considerable. For instance, the summer time-table of 1914 shows 119 Midland trains and 70 GE a day, to which should be added freight and special excursion trains. Midland services from St. Pancras at one time included trains to Norwich, but in later years, most used the

South Tottenham Station 1955

South Tottenham Station 1986

Tottenham and Forest Gate Railway to reach destinations on the London, Tilbury and Southend line. After the Second World War, for some years through passenger trains included the St. Pancras to Tilbury boat trains, with the stopping service consisting of trains from St. Pancras or Kentish Town to Barking or East

Ham. Now the only regular passenger service operates between Gospel Oak and Barking.

The first photograph was taken on a Saturday afternoon in the winter of 1955. It shows the original platforms and waiting rooms of 1871, constructed of wood to suit their position, perched on the side of the embankment. Inconsistently, although also at platform level, the gentlemen's conveniences are built of brick. A canopy was provided for eastbound passengers, perhaps on their way to Southend, but not for the smaller number of passengers awaiting trains in the St. Pancras direction. A train for Barking is approaching, consisting of former Midland Railway compartment coaches hauled by an LMS 2-6-2 tank locomotive. The No.40029 was built at Derby in 1931 and withdrawn in 1961. It was fitted with condensing gear for working on the Metropolitan Widened Lines and also with equipment for working push-pull trains. The group of waiting passengers are members of a University of London Extra-Mural class, studying railway history.

The most striking change by 1986 is the virtual disappearance of wood and its replacement by concrete or brick. Concrete had replaced wood for the platforms, the fence and the sleepers supporting the rails, while brick was used for the new waiting rooms. LNE-type lamps had given place to fluorescent lighting. All that remained unchanged was the signal box and the seats of wood and iron. (The signals had been converted from semaphore to colour light.) Instead of a six-coach steam-hauled train, passengers are about to join a two-coach diesel set. The two coaches, Nos. 53479 and 53477 were part of a series built in 1957 by Birmingham Railway Carriage and Wagon Company, with Leyland engines. Only second class accommodation was provided, but South Tottenham is unlikely ever to have enjoyed much first class patronage. The train was the 15.28 to Barking, being one of the half-hourly trains providing a service between Gospel Oak (connection to Richmond and North Woolwich service), and Barking (connection to the LTS

line). Despite the decline in the numbers of both passenger and freight trains, South Tottenham signal box remains busy.

24 Poplar Station NLR/LMSR/BR(LMR) PHC
11 November 1954/27 March 1986 TQ 380807

The original title of the North London Railway was the East and West India Docks and Birmingham Junction, and this summarises neatly its intended role of joining the docks to the London and Birmingham Railway. However, when the first section was finally completed in 1850, it connected with the London and Blackwall Railway Extension at Bow, to provide a passenger service between the North London suburbs and Fenchurch Street. The extension to the docks was opened for coal traffic in 1851, and for general goods in 1852. The whole pattern of services was changed when, in 1865, a line was opened from Dalston to a City terminus at Broad Street, although until the end of 1868, North London trains continued to work into Fenchurch Street. In fact, the use of Fenchurch Street as a City terminus for the North London was hardly justified, after the opening of Broad Street. The pattern of passenger services ran from Broad Street to Dalston, where trains rejoined the original ring route, either turning east for the East End and the dock area or in the opposite direction for the northern and western suburbs. A passenger station on the docks line was opened at Poplar in 1866. This remained the terminus for passengers until 1870, when a spur was constructed to join the London and Blackwall line, and NL trains ran on to Blackwall. The arrangement proved unsatisfactory, and in 1890, the service was cut back to Poplar which then continued to be the eastern passenger terminus of the NLR until 1944.

The first of the photographs was taken in 1954, ten years after the closure of Poplar to passenger traffic. It shows the platforms, but the building,

Poplar Station 1954

continued, and in 1954, Poplar Central signal box remained in use. However, dock traffic declined to the point at which the docks closed, and by 1981, it had all the signs of impending closure. There was certainly no sign of a future as a passenger carrying line.

By the early 1980s, firm decisions had been made for the revival of the dockland area. These included provision for passenger transport. Extension of the underground tube system was considered, but the choice fell on the far cheaper Docklands Light Railway, and the contract for its construction was let in 1984. Initially, the new line will follow the London and Blackwall Railway's route to Millwall Junction, where it divides. One branch will follow the old route through the Isle of Dogs. The other follows the NL line, through the sites of the stations at Poplar and Bow, and by a new connection on to the GE station at Stratford. The view of 1986 shows the old track and platforms at Poplar replaced, with work in progress on the new station buildings.

on the overbridge at the north end of the station, had already been demolished. This was on the East India Dock Road, and partly to avoid confusion with the GE Poplar station, the NL establishment was sometimes referred to as Poplar, East India Road. The end of passenger services in 1944 was the result of enemy action, but the final decision not to restore the Broad Street to Poplar service in 1945 reflected the decline in passenger traffic. Freight to the docks

Poplar Station 1986

The platforms are 33 yards (30 metres) long to accommodate the standard two-car trains of the Docklands Light Railway. The track is of standard gauge with steel rails on concrete sleepers. When the photograph was taken, track laying was proceeding, but the third rail, to supply power at 750V DC was not in position. When the new station opens in July 1987, it will be named All Saints, after the nearby Poplar Parish Church. Many comparative views reflect the decline of traffic and the reduction of facilities, but at Poplar the reverse has happened.

25 Dalston Junction NLR/LMSR/BR(LMR) P
20 August 1956/22 February 1964/25 March 1986/ 25 March 1986 TQ 336848

When the original North London ring route was opened in 1850, a station was provided at Kingsland to serve Dalston. This was replaced in 1865 by a station at the base of the triangular connection between the new line to Broad Street and the original route. There were three tracks on the Broad Street line until 1874, when a fourth was added on the down (west) side. At the approach to the platforms of the new Dalston Junction, the spur forming the east side of the triangle, branched off from the eastern pair of tracks. The platforms on the east side of the triangle were numbered 5 and 6, while those on the four tracks forking off to the left were Nos. 1, 2, 3 and 4. The original station buildings were on the overbridge which carried Graham Road. In 1916 the western (No. 2) pair of tracks were electrified on a four rail, low tension system. Electric traction must have been particularly welcome to the drivers of up trains, faced with a climb of 1 in 60 from Dalston Junction in a cutting up to a viaduct.

The first photograph, taken in 1956, was from platform 2/3, looking to Broad Street. Whereas the starting signal, with upper quadrant arm and metal post is normal, the 'sky-line' home signals,

Dalston Junction 1956

projecting far above the bridge are decidedly abnormal. With a height of 84 ft 6 in (24 metres), they were erected in 1886 and demolished in 1956, not long after the picture was taken. The train consists of the highly regarded Oerlikon stock, delivered between 1915 and 1923. The coaches were constructed, either by Metropolitan Cammell or the LNW Wolverton works, but the units were usually named after the manufacturer of the electrical equipment, Maschinenfabrik Oerliken of Switzerland. The coaches were regarded as being among the most pleasant and comfortable to be found in Britain, and their withdrawal, between 1954 and 1960, was regretted. The photograph of 1964 was taken from platform 4/5; the eastern side of the triangle on the right had been out of use for passenger trains since 1944, and closed to all traffic in 1966. The flower tubs make a sad contrast with the general air of abandonment.

By the time the first of the 1986 views was taken, access to platforms 4/5 was blocked and

Dalston Junction 1986

Dalston Junction 1964

Dalston Junction 1986

they were both taken from platform 2/3. All that remained of the original station were the flagstones forming the platform surface. Both the platform buildings, and the original buildings at street level had been demolished in 1970. Modest bus-type shelters now adorn the platforms. Only two tracks remain out of the original six. The second of the 1986 views was taken from about the same position as the 1956 view. During the intervening 30 years, the signal box had gone and all the semaphore signals which it operated.

The alignment of the tracks had not been changed, although the fourth rail had been removed, while only part of the crossover remained. New arrivals were the lamp post and the platform shelter — the metal tool chest seems to have undergone no change beyond rotation through 90 degress. While these four views record decline, by the time this book appears, Dalston Junction will have been abandoned.

26 Barking Station LTSR/Mid.R./LMSR/ BR(LMR)/BR(ER) GPFLHC
24 August 1957/3 April 1986 TQ 444843

Development at Barking has not been confined to its capacity to handle trains; the station buildings have also developed characteristically. When the LTS was opened to Tilbury in 1854, Barking was still a fishing village, and a small station building was provided adjoining the level crossing with East Street. A period of growth was associated with the extension of the District line steam trains over the LTS from 1902. However, as far as Barking was concerned, there was a pause. Electrification reached East Ham in 1905 and in 1906 work commenced on rebuilding Barking as a major interchange station and the terminal for the electric trains. A down loop and an up bay platform had been added in 1889, but between 1906 and 1908 the existing platforms were replaced by the four island platforms, with eight faces, which are still in use today. The level crossing was replaced by an overbridge, incorporating a new station building with easy access to all four platforms. The work was completed in 1908, the two year period being less than that taken at the end of the 1950s for the next

69

major reconstruction, associated with the electrification of the LTS lines.

Two pictures were taken on the East Street overbridge, one in 1957 and the other in 1986. The first view shows the 1908 building with its strange mixture of architectural detail. The brick facade consists of nine bays, with a symmetrical arrangement of three central windows with a blind window bay, a matching two light window and a doorway on each side. The central section is surmounted by a low parapet, but above the blind bays are Dutch style gables, which also served as chimneys. Each gable contained a distinctive design formed by variegated brick colours. The bays were separated by pilasters and all nine bays had relieving arches of dark red bricks. If the Dutch gables were calculated to reflect the connections of the LTS with East Anglia in general, and Canvey Island, with its Dutch population in particular, the ends of the buildings are harder to explain, as they were weatherboarded, with Venetian windows in the end gables. This unusual building served Barking from 1908 to 1961.

During this period, public road transport passed through three phases. First came the 1903 electric tram route of Barking Urban District Council, taken over by the London Passenger Transport Board in 1933. This became a trolley bus route in 1938. Trolley bus No.1729, which appears in the 1957 view, was one of 43, built during the War with 8 ft (2.4 m) wide bodies for use in South Africa. It proved impossible to ship them, and so they were transferred to London Transport. No.1729 was operating on route 691 from Barking Broadway via Ilford to Barkingside.

Trolley buses gave way to diesel buses and the view of 1986 shows a Leyland Titan, fleet No. T224, on route 169, which was trolley bus route 691, extended beyond Barkingside to Clayhall. The increase in road traffic is reflected in the widening of the East Street overbridge and the provision of a forecourt for the new station building. This was completed in 1961.

With the closure of the former LTS platforms at all the stations from Bromley to East Ham, inclusive, the importance of Barking as an interchange point between BR and LT services has increased. However, there are also considerable numbers of passengers arriving or departing from Barking, who use the expansive new concourse with its concrete-planked roof. The new building, unlike its predecessor, has no architectural eccentricities, but is well suited to its function. There have been no significant changes during the 25 years between its opening and the date of the second photograph. However, some of the modest terraced housing around it has been replaced by the type of modern building which appears in the background.

27 Barking   LTSR/Mid.R./LMSR/BR(LMR)/BR(ER)
1 March 1959/22 August 1960/3 April 1986 TQ 447842

The London, Tilbury and Southend was an unusual railway in a number of ways. In particular, while most small companies moved to absorption by a main line company, between 1852 and 1882 Tilbury advanced to independence. Absorption by the neighbouring Great Eastern might have been expected. However, by way of the Tottenham and Forest Gate line the Tilbury was also linked to the Midland, and it was that company who took over in 1912. When the Midland became part of the LMS, the Tilbury became an LMS outpost in LNE territory, using an LNE terminus at Fenchurch Street. (Until 1935 a few trains ran to Broad Street.) The anomaly ended in 1949 when the Tilbury line became part of the Eastern Region of British Railways.

The LTS was opened throughout in 1856 with three main sources of traffic expected. Firstly, there was passenger traffic to Gravesend, with its Rosherville Pleasure Gardens, reached via Tilbury and a ferry service; secondly, there was passenger traffic to the growing seaside resort of

Barking Station 1957

Barking Station 1986

Barking 1959

Barking 1960

Barking 1986

Southend, and finally, there was the hope of developing freight traffic to an outport for London at Thames Haven. The line was promoted jointly by the Eastern Counties and London and Blackwall Companies, and initially trains used the terminals at Shoreditch and Fenchurch Street. LTS track was reached at Forest Gate Junction, east of Stratford, and between that point and Tilbury, the original intermediate stations were at Barking, Rainham, Purfleet and Grays Thurrock. In 1858 a cut-off line was opened from the London and Blackwall extension through Bromley, Plaistow and East Ham, to Barking.

The 1880s were an important decade for the LTS. By 1882 it had acquired its own rolling stock and had become independent. In 1886 Tilbury Docks were opened, and finally, the new direct line to Southend, leaving the original line at Barking and rejoining at Pitsea was completed in 1888. The main development of the 1900s was the connection with the Metropolitan District Railway by the jointly owned Whitechapel and Bow Railway, opened in 1902. Initially, steam trains ran over existing lines, but quadrupling was completed from Bromley to Barking in 1908,

and Barking became the terminus for District line electric trains. It remained so until 1932, when the LMS quadrupled the line from Barking to Upminster, and District line electric services were extended over the new lines.

The three views were all taken from a footbridge, east of Barking station, looking towards the junction between the original line to Tilbury and the cut-off line of 1888. When the views of 1959 and 1960 were taken, work was in hand for the electrification of the LTS line, to be completed in 1962. This involved major developments at Barking, including the construction of new buildings, and of 'flyovers' and 'dive-unders' to provide for non-conflicting traffic movements for both BR and LT trains at the junctions to the east and to the west of the station. In the first view, temporary tracks have been laid for direct Southend trains, leaving the space in the centre of the picture free for the construction of a new dive-under for LT trains. The Southend train using the temporary line consists of a standard BR 2-6-4T locomotive, No.80071, hauling a mixture of ex-LMS and BR compartment coaches. No.80071 had a short life, for it was built at Brighton Works in 1953, and withdrawn in 1964.

By August 1960, when the second picture was taken, the dive-under was completed, and the direct line to Southend had been restored. LT trains were using the new alignments, and the rear of a Wimbledon train can be seen disappearing into the dive-under. (At this date, LT electric trains still carried oil tail lamps.) Barking East signal box of 1908 is still in position and work on the new station building is continuing on the bridge in the right background. Masts have been erected in preparation for the electrification of the LTS line. By 1986, this had been in use for 24 years. The signal box has been demolished, although a platelayers' hut, newly constructed in 1960, is still in use. The rear of a Richmond train is disappearing into the underpass. Although on balance, the 1960s were a period of decline on many parts of the railways, as the views at Barking show, there were patches of development.

28 Plaistow LTSR/Mid.R./LMSR/BR(LMR)/BR(ER) GPFLHC

16 August 1956/27 March 1986 TQ 397832

Plaistow Station was opened on the LTS cut-off line between Bromley and Barking, as mentioned above. In 1869, a spur was opened from Bow, NL, to Bromley, LTS, and a service was provided to and from the North London line until 1916. This included through coaches and some through trains to Southend, while from 1871 the regular shuttle service terminated in a bay platform at Plaistow. Trains of a third company were to be seen from 1902, when, with the opening of the Whitechapel and Bow line, Metropolitan District trains ran on to the LTS. Plaistow was rebuilt with four through-platforms and terminal bays on both sides of the station, the work being completed in 1905. The North London service ended at the beginning of 1916. After the LTS electrification, BR trains ceased to call, and Plaistow was served exclusively by LT electric trains. The down side bay is used by the occasional LT train which terminates at Plaistow. In addition to passenger traffic, Plaistow had its own goods depot and also extensive marshalling yards for the breaking down or making up of freight trains for the LTS. The locomotive and carriage works and the original locomotive depot were situated immediately to the north of the station.

London's sewage problems were relieved by 1868 when the Northern Outfall Sewer was completed between Abbey Mills Pumping Station and the Thames at Barking, crossing over the LTS to the west of Plaistow station. It was well above ground level and provided the viewpoint for the photographs of 1956 and 1986. The original engine shed and the works were both closed by 1956. Heavy repairs were transferred to Derby after the Midland took over. However, the buildings were leased to the car company, Volkswagen, and the basic structures were unchanged. The rebuilding of the end of the left hand section of the former running shed was

Plaistow 1956

necessitated by bomb damage. A new shed, originally known as West Ham, was built on the opposite side of the sewage outfall and the three enginemen in the 1956 view, are going off duty from that shed. The semaphore signal, points, and a number of ground signals were operated by wires and rodding from the signal box, erected in 1905. To the right are the extensive up side marshalling yards, which, together with the down yards on the far side of the sewer, were replaced in the early 1960s, by new yards at Ripple Lane, east of Barking. The up stopping train in the 1956 view is being hauled by a Stanier 2-6-4T, built at Derby in 1934. No.42504 was one of a series of 37 locomotives, specially designed for the Tilbury line with three cylinders instead of two, as this decreased the hammer blow on the viaduct approaching Fenchurch Street. Until nationalisation, the structure was the property of the LNE, whose civil engineer might have taken exception to excessive strain from LMS locomotives. No.42504 was withdrawn when the LTS was electrified in 1962. Locomotives on the Tilbury line were not turned at the termini; instead it was usual for them to run down to Southend chimney first, and to return bunker first, although a journey via Tilbury would have upset this arrangement.

Plaistow 1986

The view of 1986 shows many changes. Flats, a roadway and garages have replaced the marshalling yard. The signal box was demolished in 1961, having ceased to control trains from 1959. The only points to be seen are for the LT tracks to the terminal bay. A somewhat unexpected survival is the wooden lamp post in the right foreground. This is less explicable than the spreading of the tracks to pass under the Northern Outfall Sewer. The old running sheds and the works were swept away in the 1970s to be replaced by new buildings. An eastbound LT electric train is just visible in the left foreground, while two four-coach electric units of class 305 form the LTS up fast train. There is little to show that Plaistow was once an important railway centre.

Finsbury Park Station 1955

Finsbury Park Station 1959

29 Finsbury Park Station GNR/LNER/BR(ER) P
2 July 1955/17 January 1959/25 March 1986
TQ 314868

The Great Northern line was opened in 1850: it extended from a temporary London terminus in Maiden Lane, near Kings Cross, to as far north as Peterborough. By 1861, the Great Northern was beginning to develop suburban traffic and opened a station, 2½ miles (4 km) from Kings Cross, named Seven Sisters Road, Holloway. This was changed to Finsbury Park in 1869. With the opening of branches to Edgware, High Barnet and Alexandra Palace and of the spur to the North London line, Finsbury Park became an important junction and interchange point — a Clapham Junction of North London. Provision for passengers changing trains was made by a footbridge in 1867, replaced by a subway opened in 1874. The subway was enlarged in 1889 and supplemented by a second subway in 1894. Trains from the GN reached the City at Broad Street (North London Railway) and Moorgate (Metropolitan Railway), but finally the GN, perhaps inspired by the LSW tube line from

Finsbury Park Station 1986

Waterloo to the Bank, was associated with the Great Northern and City Railway, a tube line from Finsbury Park to Moorgate. This was opened in 1904 and could accommodate main line trains. (An LSW equivalent would have been a line from Clapham Junction to the Bank, which also took main line stock.)

The network of subways under Finsbury Park was extended to serve entrances to Station Place, Seven Sisters Road, Wells Terrace and to the GN and C. A second tube line, the Great Northern, Piccadilly and Brompton reached Finsbury Park in 1906. The 1935 London Transport new works plan envisaged the GN & C and the GN North London branches being absorbed into the LT Northern line network; work was begun on this project, including the foundations for a surface platform at Finsbury Park. After the end of the war, this was abandoned. In the next phase of London Transport development, completed between 1965 and 1968 the Finsbury Park tube platforms of the GN and City and the GN, Piccadilly and Brompton were used by trains of the Piccadilly and of the newly opened Victoria line. In 1976, the remainder of the GN and City was transferred to British Rail and used as a City line for trains from the Great Northern, as anticipated when it was first built.

To some degree, evidence of the complicated history of Finsbury Park has been expunged by modernisation. The views of 1955, 1959 and 1986 all taken from the country end of platform 7, reflect something of the changes that have taken place since the end of the war. Appearing in all three views, without significant change, are the platform, the line and the girders of the bridge over Stroud Green Road. The signal post, viewed in 1955 and 1959, was placed on a bracket to avoid it being obscured by platform canopies, and carried three arms, indicating the route to be followed. In 1986, a colour light signal with direction indicators fulfilled this function. Finsbury Park No. 5 signal box, with its gable end outlined with bargeboards, reflected former GN ownership. Other features in the view of 1955 are

the water crane and the fogman's hut. The 1959 view includes a gentlemen's convenience and the canopy of Platform 6. All these had gone by 1986, when new features included the lamps with station names, the loudspeakers of the public address system and the concrete tubs for flowers. While all these changes are significant, perhaps the most striking developments are to be found in the provision of an overhead electric traction supply. In 1955, the down train is being hauled by a steam locomotive, No.61097, one of the 274 locomotives built between 1942 and 1952 of the 4-6-0 B1 Class. No.61097 was built by the North British Locomotive Company in 1946 and was withdrawn in 1965. By 1959, diesel power had been introduced, and haulage was provided by No. D5308, re-numbered to 26009 in 1968. Class 26 consisted of 47 locomotives built by the Birmingham Railway Carriage and Wagon Company in 1958, and scrapped between 1977 and 1983. The end of the leading coach, of typical LNE pannelled construction, includes the guard's lookout, and a destination indicator turned to 'Hertford North'. The 1986 view shows an electric multiple unit train, running between Kings Cross and Royston. Unit No.312724 belonged to Class 312, built for the electrification of services from Kings Cross in 1977, and working from Hornsey Depot. Apart from main line trains with diesel power, all trains to be seen at Finsbury Park are now electric.

30 Palmers Green GNR/LNER/BR(ER) GP
c.1904/25 March 1986 TQ 309927

By the end of the 1860s, London suburban traffic was providing a significant proportion of the revenue of the Great Northern Company, and in 1871 this was augmented by the opening of a new railway from the main line at Wood Green to Enfield. While Enfield itself was served by the Eastern Counties Railway from 1849, the new GN route penetrated countryside 'ripe for develop-

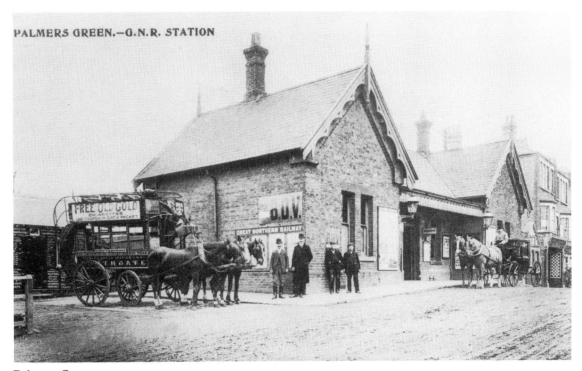

PALMERS GREEN.—G.N.R. STATION

Palmers Green 1904

ment'. One of its original stations was opened on Alderman's Hill to serve Palmers Green. Development was slow, and in a bid to extend the catchment area of the station, in 1876, the GN renamed it 'Palmers Green and Southgate'. (It returned to Palmers Green in 1971, its centenary year.) By 1932, new housing had spread over the fields but unfortunately for Palmers Green Station, this was the year in which the London Underground Group extended its Piccadilly line from Finsbury Park to Cockfosters, with a station at Southgate. Frequent electric trains, running through to central London, won traffic from the steam trains of the former GN line, then running to Hertford North. When electrification finally reached the GN in 1976, a frequent service was provided between Moorgate and Hertford, with many trains running through to Welwyn Garden City, and Palmers Green revived.

The first photograph, taken about 1904, shows the station in the era of steam railways and horse-drawn road transport. The bus connection for Southgate, drawn by three horses, waits at the end of the station buildings, while for the more affluent, a two-horse cab is drawn up at the front. (The lavish provision of horse power reflects steep slopes on some of the local roads.) In a period before mechanical propulsion on the roads, the surface has not been made up, but remains suitable for the hoofs of horses. The station buildings were built alongside the road bridge, over the railway, and housed the booking office and waiting rooms, but not the station master. The symmetrical gables are adorned with bargeboards and finials, of the type often provided on GN stations and signal boxes. A canopy, with vallance, covers the entrance between the two gable ended bays. Gas lamps are supported by brackets, and enamel advertise-ments and billboards are fixed to the walls. The tall chimneys suggest blazing coal fires.

In the 1986 photograph, the building has

Palmers Green 1986

changed little. The bargeboards have been simplified and the chimneys shortened, but the windows and drainpipe look much the same. However, the gas lamps and the advertisements have been removed, while a new sign occupies one of the gable ends. Corresponding to the horse bus, are motor buses on London Transport's route 29, which covered the road between

Palmers Green and Southgate. Missing from the Edwardian view was private transport, represented in 1986 by motor cars. The yard and office at the side of the station, once occupied by Walker and Son, jobmasters, was no longer in transport use. The new road surface reflects the change from horse to mechanical road transport. Perhaps the most surprising feature is the way in which the station buildings, designed for 1871, are still operative in 1986.

FOUR

South East London and beyond

South east London was traversed by the main lines of the LBSC, SE and LCD companies. Each of them forked to serve both City and West End terminals, the LBSC as far out as Croydon, the LCD at Herne Hill and SE at Borough Market Junction, on the City side of London Bridge Station. The pattern was complicated by subsidiary through lines, such as the Mid-Kent and North Kent lines of the SE, or the Catford loop of the LCD. There were also branch lines such as the SE to Bromley and the LCD to Crystal Palace. One of the most distinctive features of the railway pattern in the south east sector was the construction of competing routes by main line companies. Three branch lines — the SE to Bromley, the LCD to Crystal Palace, and the LCD to Greenwich — all had terminals in places served by other companies. (It is perhaps significant that part of the Greenwich branch and all of the Crystal Palace branch have been closed.) Bricklayer's Arms was closed as a London terminal for passengers in 1851, and has now been closed to goods. Whereas in the south west, Nine Elms served as both a land terminal and a riverside wharf, in the south east there were separate riverside wharves: for the LCD at Blackfriars, for the LBSC at Deptford Wharf and for the SE at Angerstein's Wharf. Of these, only the track to Angerstein's Wharf at Charlton remains, but for private siding rather than riverborne traffic.

During the building boom between the wars, the Southern, with their policy of electrification supported by the close network inherited from the pre-grouping companies, did not suffer competition from underground lines in this area.

Their only penetration was over the long established East London line, which also carried steam-hauled freight trains from the GE system. These ran through to the principal marshalling yard at Hither Green, but have been discontinued. Whereas one of the great changes north of the river has been the demise of docks traffic, there has been no equivalent change, as the Surrey Commercial Docks, the only dock system on the south side, always relied mainly on road and on water transport. Since the war, consolidation has been more notable than radical development, although there have been two closures of passenger-carrying lines. Mainly because of the changes in the journey to work pattern, both geographical and modal, there has been some decline in the more local traffic, with an increase in longer distance through traffic. However, compared to the great development of suburban traffic between the wars, the period since has been relatively stable.

Abbreviations

BR(SR)	British Railways (Southern Region)
ELR	East London Railway (GE, LBSC, MD, Met., LCD and SE)
LBSCR	London, Brighton and South Coast Railway
LCDR	London, Chatham and Dover Railway
SR	Southern Railway
SER	South Eastern Railway
SECR	South Eastern and Chatham Managing Committee

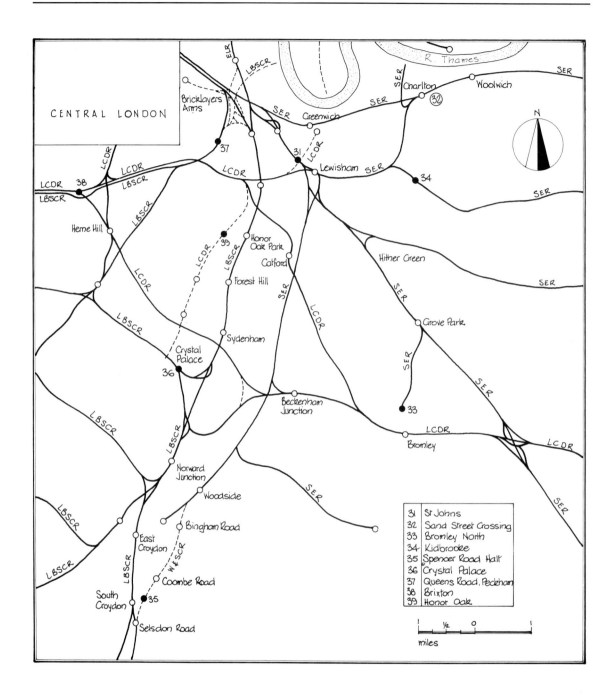

CENTRAL LONDON

R. Thames

Bricklayers Arms

Charlton
Woolwich
Greenwich
Lewisham
Herne Hill
Honor Oak Park
Catford
Hither Green
Forest Hill
Grove Park
Sydenham
Crystal Palace
Beckenham Junction
Bromley
Norwood Junction
Woodside
Bingham Road
East Croydon
Coombe Road
South Croydon
Selsdon Road

31	St Johns
32	Sand Street Crossing
33	Bromley North
34	Kidbrooke
35	Spencer Road Halt
36	Crystal Palace
37	Queens Road, Peckham
38	Brixton
39	Honor Oak

½   0

miles

W&SCR   Woodside and South Croydon
Railway (LBSC & SE)

Undertakings in bold lettering in the main took over from the original companies. There were two stages — take over by the 'Big Four' in 1923, and then take over by British Railways in 1948.

31 St. John's SER/SECR/SR/BR(SR) P
12 March 1955/2 July 1976 TQ 375763

Some main lines, such as the London and Birmingham, were built in one stage, but others, such as the SE main line to Dover, evolved over a period. The first section was the London and Greenwich of 1836. Trains ran on over the London and Croydon, shared the London and Brighton route as far as Redhill, and then followed their own line via Tonbridge across the Kentish weald to Dover. This route was completed in 1844. Five years later an important new line was opened via Lewisham and Woolwich to Gravesend, known as the North Kent line. With the onslaught of LCD competition, the SE decided to improve its route to Dover, by using the North Kent route to a

junction just short of Lewisham and then constructing a new line through the North Downs to join the original line at Tonbridge. The North Kent was quadrupled as far as the junction, and in 1873, a station opened on the London side of the junction. Like the cut-off line to Dover, the new station, named St. John's after a nearby church, was a response to LCD competition — in this case a station which LCD had opened at Lewisham Road in 1871 on the LCD line to Greenwich.

When the first photograph was taken in 1955, the station comprised two island platforms in a wide cutting. Only passenger traffic was accommodated; the sidings behind the fence on the left were not used for handling freight. Using the additional space provided by the wide cutting, instead of placing the station building over the running lines, it was offset to the end of the sidings. St. John's Road crossed over the railway at the London end of the station, and the modest building, timberframed and weatherboarded with a slate roof, was sited at street level, with a footbridge giving access to the platforms. Other features shown in the 1955 view are the flat-bottomed track, the SR concrete lamp posts and the overhead telegraph lines on pairs of tall poles. Local trains had been electrified from 1926, but the expresses for the Kent Coast line were still worked by steam. The down express shown in the photograph is being hauled by a Battle of Britain

St John's 1955

St John's 1976

Class locomotive, No.34081, built at Brighton Works for British Railways in 1948. It was withdrawn in 1964.

The major developments of the early seventies to increase the capacity of the lines into London Bridge were complete by the time of the second view in 1976. At St. John's, the western island platform, which served the fast lines was demolished, and the sidings were removed. The space gained was occupied by an embankment, carrying a new spur from the line linking Lewisham to the LCD system. This was, in effect, part of a flyover, enabling trains from the Dartford direction to reach the up fast line without obstructing the slow line. The height of the embankment necessitated the construction of a new footbridge between the station building and the surviving island platform. It will be seen that the new arrangements of 1975 did not lead to any changes in the island platform on the slow lines. The Kent Coast expresses had been electrically worked since 1961 and the rear four-coach unit on the up Ramsgate and Dover express, is formed of a 4-BEP unit (BR class 410/2), built at Eastleigh and delivered in 1959. The changes at St. John's particularly reflect investment in services to the south east in the early seventies.

32 Sand Street Crossing SER/SECR/SR/BR(SR)
24 December 1954/27 March 1986 TQ 421789

One of the changes noted during the last 30 years has been the virtual elimination of the traditional level crossing. This was expensive to operate and maintain, and when closure was not possible, automatic or remote-controlled barriers replaced gates. In central London, busy streets came before the railways, which were either constructed above or below ground level. The North Kent line of the SER was opened in 1849, and outside the built up areas, where the line ran at street level, crossings were provided. Most of them were to be found where the line crossed flat land near the River Thames, and the first group were built between Charlton and Woolwich. Sand Street crossing was on the western edge of Woolwich, near the tunnel under what became Maryon Park. In the early days, the gates were operated by crossing keepers who were provided with dwellings adjoining the gates, comparable to the lodge houses which controlled access to the great estates, or to tollhouses on the roads.

When the view at Sand Street was taken in 1954, the original crossing keeper's house of 1849 survived, although it was no longer connected with the working of the crossing. An early development to assist crossing keepers in

Sand Street Crossing 1954

Sand Street Crossing 1986

ascertaining whether or not trains were due, was the provision of telegraphic communication with neighbouring signal boxes. At busy crossings the next step was the erection of a cabin, connected to the neighbouring signal boxes, from which the gates could be operated by wire ropes, driven by a large manually operated wheel. Sand Street was still at this stage in 1954, and the wheel can be seen through the nearest window. The gates have a locking mechanism, worked from the cabin, and the opening and closing of the gate is interlocked with protective signals, which could not be pulled off to allow the passage of trains unless the gates were closed to road traffic. Although practice varied, in the London area most of the crossings were usually kept open for road traffic and only closed across the roads to permit the passage of trains.

At many crossings, separate wicket gates were provided for pedestrians. Unlike the road gates, these could not block the railway, and they were operated by the pedestrians who used them. They were left open later than the main gates, but were usually locked just before the arrival of a train. When the photograph of 1954 was taken, the road gates had already been closed, but the lady with the shopping was about to pass through the wicket gate. In some cases, footbridges were provided instead of wicket gates, but this was not done at Sand Street, perhaps because of the proximity of a footbridge separate from the crossing. It is worth noting that the crossing box had no part in the control of railway traffic, its role of ensuring that the crossing was reserved either for rail or for road traffic being strictly passive.

In 1954, the box, typical of SE construction with its weatherboarding, sash windows and slate roof, and the gas light above the wicket gate, all belonged to the Victorian railway scene. By 1986, change was complete, and the only connection between the two views is the track, and the concrete footbridge in the background. The crossing has been closed to road traffic and fenced off, although the break in the pavement shows where the road once ran. The overhead telegraph line has been replaced, and the box and adjoining dwelling have been demolished. Not only the crossing, but also the surrounding streets have been altered, terraced housing shown in the first view being replaced by tower blocks with a new street pattern. The crossing keepers knew their 'regular customers', and the closure of crossing boxes has removed a point of contact between railway workers and the public.

33 Bromley North Station SER/SECR/SR/BR(SR) GPFL
1921/1926/18 April 1986 *TQ 403698*

The LCD station at Bromley was opened in 1858 on what became the main line. A local branch was opened from the SE main line at Grove Park in 1878 with one intermediate station at Sundridge Park. The extent to which the terminal station was planned for local passengers is reflected in the lack of provision for horse and carriage traffic. The view of 1921 shows a typical SE timber-framed, weatherboarded building with a slate roof. A modest canopy welcomes passengers, and the Bell Telephone Company sign indicates the availability to the public of one of their instruments. Both the station master's dwelling and the goods office were separate buildings. The original goods office appears in the right foreground, with overflow accommodation in the adapted coach body visible beyond the canopy. Other signs of goods traffic are the two delivery vans and the top of the crane above the left hand van. By the advent of the Southern in 1923, both passenger and freight traffic had grown sufficiently to require new buildings.

By this time, the competition between the LCD and SE had lapsed for at least 27 years, and as there was no longer any possibility of the SE branch extending, the new station was built across the end of the line. In the same vein, the SE station had become Bromley North and the LCD Bromley South. The Southern, during the 25 years of its existence, had two styles of architecture, one for the 1920s and another for the 1930s. In the 1930s a consciously modern style, almost suggestive of a cinema was favoured, stations such as Wimbledon and Surbiton being representative. For the 1920s, a more conservative style, suggestive of more elegant classical buildings and of banks was chosen, as at Ramsgate or Bromley North. The Bromley North building incor-porated a pediment and was surmounted by a cupola. According to the general manager, Sir Herbert Walker, stations were the shop windows of the railway, and this precept was extended by incorporating shops to let in the new building. (They appear on the right hand side.) This was completed in 1925, and by the time the second photograph was taken, the branch had been electrified — a notice board proclaims 'Southern Electric'. Other marks of the newly formed company are a poster showing 'Sunny South Sam', a mythical guard who promoted the holiday image of the company and the words 'Southern Railway' engraved in stone over the entrance. Signs evocative of the period are fixed to the gas lamp post: 'To London 9½ M' and an A.A. direction sign to the 'Motor Park'. In front,

Bromley North Station 1921

Bromley North Station 1926

Bromley North Station 1986

on a black and white striped pole is a speed restriction sign. House agents often had offices adjoining suburban stations and the notice of Messrs Carter, Law and Leech appears at the extreme right.

Perhaps the most striking feature of the view of 1986 is that after about 60 years, the station shows so little change. Following the closure to goods traffic in 1968, the goods and parcels office, which appears on the left in the 1926 view, was demolished, and most of the shops have changed hands. Yet the commuter of the 1920s would not feel too out of place in the 1986 station. The setting, however, is a very different matter, with an elaborate traffic system in the forecourt and a large office block on the left.

34 Kidbrooke Station SER/SECR/SR/BR(SR) G*P *1918/1 March 1980* TQ 409757

The Bexley Heath Railway company was planned to develop the country between the South Eastern's North Kent and Dartford loop lines. When the South Eastern finally realised that if they did not incorporate the line into their system, the London, Chatham and Dover might, they agreed to work the new line. It was opened in 1895 with severe gradients and sharp curves, as it was not intended to carry through trains. Mainly to accommodate traffic that would arise if the Earl of St. Germans should develop his estate, a station was opened by the bridge carrying Kidbrooke Park Road. The anticipated building did not take place, but in 1917 a large military supply depot was built on the south side of the station. By 1918, this had become the RAF No.1 stores depot, associated with an RAF camp on the north side. The depot brought both passenger and freight traffic to Kidbrooke until, after a period of decline, it finally closed in 1967. Meanwhile, in 1926 the Bexleyheath line was electrified, and some of the long delayed housing development had occurred.

The first view was taken from the road bridge, probably late in the afternoon of a day in the summer of 1918. The original wooden station buildings of 1895, with booking office and waiting room on the up side, and a small shelter on the down side, had not been altered. The unpaved platforms are lit by gas lamps and are carrying far more passengers than could have been foreseen in the most optimistic hopes of the Bexley Heath directors. It is clearly evening rush hour at the depot, and the passengers, mostly hatted, are pouring on to the up platform to

Kidbrooke Station 1918

return to their homes in the London suburbs. A few have crossed by the road bridge and are waiting on the down platform for journeys in the direction of Eltham and Bexley Heath. A South Eastern 4-4-0 locomotive of the B1 class is simmering gently at the end of the marshalling yard, to the right of the station building.

Much had changed by 1980. The running lines appear in the same position, but continuous welded rail with a live rail for electric trains, supported by concrete sleepers, has replaced traditional railway track. The platforms are paved, and the ornate gas lamps have given place to electric lights on steel poles. Chain link fencing with wooden rails occupies the site of the original wooden palings. A concrete footbridge has removed the need for passengers to cross over the line by walking back to the road bridge. There is nothing to be seen of the marshalling yard, closed after the First World War, with the depot traffic passing through new exchange sidings, on the opposite side of the road bridge, and more conveniently supervised from Kidbrooke signal box. The new station buildings of 1972 had been built in response to a large housing development

Kidbrooke Station 1980

on the site of the RAF supply depot. It would now take an effort of the imagination to recall a platform filled with war workers in 1918.

35 Spencer Road Halt W & SC (LBSC & SE)/SR/ BR(SR) P*
1922/21 December 1955/1 April 1986 TQ 334644

Various plans for new lines to serve the country between the LBSC and SE main lines, authorized in the 1860s, had been thwarted by the financial problems of the latter part of that decade. Most of them were revived in the 1880s, including a joint line from Croydon to Oxted. This was reached from the LBSC main line at South Croydon and from the SE Mid Kent line at Woodside, the connections joining at Selsdon Road.

The joint lines were opened in 1885, with the section between Woodside and Selsdon Road being the responsibility of the Woodside and South Croydon joint committee. Although built for through traffic, the line, which was just over 2¼ miles (3½ km) long, was provided with one intermediate station at Coombe Lane. The Bexleyheath line was built for local traffic but acquired some through traffic. The Woodside and South Croydon was built for through traffic but did acquire a certain amount of local traffic. To develop this, a steam rail motor car service was introduced in 1906, and halts were opened at Bingham Road and Spencer Road. Both halts and Coombe Lane Station were closed in the First World War, but the line remained open for through traffic. In view of the proximity of other stations, particularly South Croydon, it is somewhat surprising that in 1935 the Woodside and South Croydon was electrified. Coombe Lane Station and Bingham Road Halt were re-

Spencer Road Halt 1922

Spencer Road Halt 1955

opened, but, in view of its being only about a quarter of a mile from South Croydon Station, Spencer Road was not reinstated. An application was made to close the line in 1963 but in the event, it remained open until 1983.

Spencer Road was closed in 1915, but when the first photograph was taken in 1922, it remained intact. Since the opening of the line, South Croydon had expanded with the type of housing which was likely to produce season ticket

Spencer Road Halt 1986

holders. The underbridge crossing Croham Road is visible and beyond it, the up starter signal of Selsdon Road. The footbridge, from which the view was taken, preserved a right of way when the railway was built in 1885. The platforms are reached from either side of the bridge, and the halt is named after nearby Spencer Road. The notice adjoining the gate, headed 'Woodside and South Croydon Railway' warns pedestrians against taking a short cut over the railway instead of using the bridge. Apart from the probable provision of oil lamps, Spencer Road appears to have consisted of nothing beyond platforms and nameboards.

The second view, taken on a misty day in the winter of 1955, shows the site after the electrification of the line and its re-opening to local traffic. A Southern Railway signal post, made of old rails, carries the Selsdon Road starter in a new position and the telegraph pole has acquired more wires. The site of the down platform is occupied by a war time tank trap. Concrete fencing has replaced wood, but the footbridge remains unchanged. An up electric train is approaching. The third view was taken in 1986,

nearly three years after the closure of the line. The third rail and the signal arm have been removed and the fencing is damaged; but apart from this, the main change is due to thirty years' growth of vegetation. There is now nothing left of one of London's shorter lived stations.

36 Crystal Palace Station   LBSCR/SR/BR(SR) GPLHC
September 1913/21 March 1964/18 April 1986
TQ 342705

One of the milestones in the history of the nineteenth century was the Great Exhibition of 1851, with its Crystal Palace in Hyde Park. The Crystal Palace was purchased and re-erected in an enlarged form on the crest of a hill at Sydenham. The promoters included members of the LBSC Board and, not surprisingly, a branch line was opened in 1854 from the Brighton main line at Sydenham to the foot of the hill to serve the new centre. An extension with a tunnel under the hill was completed in 1856 to give a connection to west London. Finally, in 1857, a third line was opened, giving access to the Palace from the south and east, with a junction with the original line on the London side of the station. (For a while this was used by main line trains from Kent to the West End.) The 1857 line had separate platforms forming an annexe, on the south side of the main Crystal Palace station. Major events at the Palace brought heavy traffic to the station, despite competition from a rival LCD establishment from 1865. In 1911 electric trains were introduced, using the Brighton's overhead system, which was replaced with the Southern's third rail in 1929. A disastrous fire destroyed the Palace in 1936, and although the grounds remain in use, it has never regained its Victorian pre-

Crystal Palace Station 1913

Crystal Palace Station 1964

eminence as an entertainment centre. The LCD station was closed in 1954, and the LBSC station has undergone a degree of rationalisation.

All three views were taken from the same point on the platforms outside the main station. These consisted of up and down platforms serving through lines and a third platform with two dead-end tracks. In the 1913 view, one of the terminal tracks is being used by a motor train of two coaches, with the locomotive in the middle. As indicated by the gantries, the line to Norwood Junction and the south has been electrified, but the steam train would have provided a shuttle service to Beckenham Junction for eastward bound passengers. A side wall of the main station is prominent in the background, one section with blind arcading, and the other with buttresses. The roofline of the ornate buildings at street level, including a roof so steeply pitched as to form a turret, is striking.

By 1964, the most apparent visual change is the substitution of the third rail for overhead wire electrification. Lighting was still by gas, but with different lamps, including concrete posts on the up platform. The only change visible in the buildings is the canopy over the up platform. A 4-EPB electric multiple unit train was running in on the down through platform.

In 1986, there are many more changes. On the skyline, a transmitting mast has appeared, while the turret, forming part of the station, has gone, having been demolished in 1976. The turret did have statutory protection but, after gale force winds, it was considered unsafe. A new entrance and booking hall, with curved ribs suggesting the original Crystal Palace are under construction alongside the original Victorian building. The lamp posts have been replaced, but more striking is the abolition of the terminal platforms. As in 1964, an electric multiple unit train is approaching, in this case No.6304, one of the 1951 2-EPB sets refurbished to form part of class 416 in 1982. It was running between Victoria and Beckenham Junction. The 'annexe' is more interesting than impressive, but the main building at Crystal Palace is the finest Victorian station in south London.

Crystal Palace Station 1986

37 Queen's Road, Peckham LBSCR/SR/BR(SR)
c.1922/27 March 1986 *TQ 350767*

Most of the comparative views have been taken on railway property, but clearly railway development is visible from many other places. Views were taken from the southern pavement of Queen's Road, Peckham in 1922 and 1986. Both show the bridge carrying the railway over the road, and the 1922 view includes the end of the station. The line and the station were opened in 1866, forming part of the South London line, electrified on an overhead system between Victoria and London Bridge in 1909. It also carried through traffic from London Bridge to Sutton, Horsham and beyond and somewhat

Queen's Road Peckham 1922

Queen's Road Peckham 1986

unusually, was provided with three tracks. Substitution of a live rail for overhead wire occurred in 1928, and in 1933, the centre track was taken out of use and subsequently removed.

The 1922 view shows the extent to which the railway companies exploited all well-placed, vertical surfaces for advertising. An advertisement for Nestlé's tinned milk occupies the parapet of the bridge, a firm of undertakers have a place on the end of the abutment, and the advertising selection at the back of the station platform includes toffees, cigarettes and whisky. The LBSC itself was not left out, with a sign showing the way to the station entrance, and a bold announcement on the bridge: 'Elevated Electric. Trains every few minutes. Victoria in 17 minutes. Crystal Palace in 18 minutes. London Bridge in 5 minutes. Brixton in 6 minutes'. The end of the wooden station building, a signal post and a gantry supporting the overhead wires are all visible. The road surface consists of granite setts, and illumination is by gas lamps. Of special interest is the London County Council tramway line, with electric current collected from live rails carried in a conduit and reached through a slot. (The view shows both live rail electrification for trams and overhead electrification for trains.)

In 1986 the granite setts are buried under a blacktop surface. The trams ceased to run in 1952, and whereas the 1922 view showed public transport in the form of a bus, a tram and a lorry, the 1986 view shows a preponderance of private motor cars. For lighting, gas has given way to electricity and the small lamps have been replaced by tall steel posts. On the railway, after the removal of the third track, Queen's Road Station was left with a large gap between the outer tracks. When deterioration of the wooden platforms and buildings necessitated their replacement, a new island platform was built on the site of the third track in 1974. The posts supporting white boards shown on the left in the 1986 photograph were designed to prevent passengers alighting into space instead of onto the new island platform. Two new spans on modified

abutments have replaced the original bridge. A sign indicating the position of the station entrance, bearing the BR logo, is in roughly the same place as the 1922 sign, but the adjacent advertisement listing BR property to let, together with the proclamations of the furniture and bedding centre under the arch, tends to swamp it. The only railway feature virtually unchanged, except for the bridge abutment, is the end of the viaduct.

38 Brixton Station   LCDR/SECR/SR/BR(SR)   P
1930/*1 April 1986*   *TQ 312756*

In the early 1860s, the newly formed London, Chatham and Dover Company, having opened in Kent, was extending into London. From a junction at Herne Hill, one line ran north to the City and another took a north westerly route to the West End. The latter was opened, with a station at Brixton, in 1862. A third line was opened in 1863, from a junction just west of Brixton Station, running in an easterly direction, and enabling trains from the West End to reach the City. Unlike the LBSC Victoria and London Bridge Service, which is still running, the LCD trains were withdrawn in 1916. They ran between Victoria and Holborn Viaduct or Moorgate, on what was known as the Metropolitan Extension service.

Both the photographs were taken from the Victoria end of Brixton, on the main line side. (The junction for the City, now mainly used by trains running via the Catford loop or to the SE lines is visible in the view of 1930.) The first view shows the junction operated mechanically with semaphore signals from a substantial signal box, built of brick with a projecting window. The up signals for both the main and the City lines consist of metal lattice posts with brackets, lower quadrant arms and finials. On each post there are stop signals and pairs of distants to indicate which

Brixton Station 1930

Brixton Station 1986

of the two up lines on the three track section from Shepherd's Lane Junction was to be used; a treadle is visible on the down main line. The third rail had been in use for electric trains since 1925. The platforms on the City line were disused. The fence on the up side consisted of concrete panels, while the iron railings on the down side carried both enamel advertisements and bill boards. Confirmation of the period is provided by the lady's costume, particularly the fur, slung over her right shoulder. Both up and down trains are signalled for the City line, and the down train, consisting of empty main line stock hauled by an unidentified tank locomotive, is approaching the junction.

In the photograph of 1986, the only signal visible is a colour light at the end of the platform. The signal box adjoining the junction was closed in 1959, at the time of the Kent Coast electrification, and its work transferred to Shepherd's Lane signal box. On the platforms, steel lamp posts with fluorescent lights have replaced the adapted gas lamp posts, seen in the first view. The temporary cabinets were associated with the general refurbishment and upgrading of Brixton, to include statuary and other works of art, financed by the Greater London Council. In view of risks from bombing and redevelopment, it is remarkable that most of the buildings in the 1930s view, including Marks and Spencer's and the Bon Marché, also appear in the 1986 photograph. However, part of the parapet of the bridge over Brixton Road is being replaced. The train on the down main line is the 15.20 from Victoria to Ramsgate, with set 1591 approaching the camera. When constructed at Eastleigh in 1957, this was a 4-CEP unit, rebuilt in 1979 to class 411/5. Although main line express trains still pass through Brixton, they may be felt to lack the charisma of, for instance, the steam-hauled 'Golden Arrow'. However, the station itself, upgraded through its proximity to a new cultural centre, is now ornamented with works of art which would hardly have been contemplated in times past.

39 Honor Oak Station LCDR/SECR/SR/BR(SR) GP
1922/14 September 1954/21 March 1964
TQ 351741

The dramatic expansion of the London, Chatham and Dover Railway company in the early 1860s involved not only new through routes, but also the acquisition of lines designed for London traffic. The Crystal Palace and South London Junction was opened in 1865, and was operated and later absorbed by the LCD. Its large station at the Crystal Palace was better placed than that of the LBSC, which had been opened 11 years earlier. Not only at the Palace, but throughout its length, the LCD line was within half a mile of an LBSC main line and was therefore always subject to competition. By the 1880s all the stations were in pairs — the two at Crystal Palace, Upper Sydenham (LCD) with Sydenham (LBSC) Lordship Lane (LCD) with Forest Hill (LBSC), and Honor Oak (LCD) with Honor Oak Park (LBSC). Because of this, it is not surprising that the LCD Crystal Palace line was closed in both World Wars, from 1917 to 1919 and again from 1944 to 1946. More surprising is its electrification in 1925, but at this time, although Crystal Palace traffic was already declining, commuting from the inner suburbs was increasing. However, under post-war conditions, traffic was insufficient, and the LCD line to Crystal Palace was finally closed in 1954.

Honor Oak was opened in 1865, with its platforms on an embankment adjoining the bridge over Forest Hill Road. The station master's detached house and the station offices were built at ground level on the down side and wooden shelters were provided on the wooden platforms. The first view was taken in 1922 from the down platform, looking towards Nunhead. An up train, with a bird cage lookout for the guard visible on the rear coach, has just passed the starter signal. Apart from the mantles of the gas lamps and the enamel advertisements, the platforms have apparently changed little since

Honor Oak Station 1922

Honor Oak Station 1954

Honor Oak Station 1964

1865. From the booking office a subway runs under the embankment, with flights of stairs up to the platforms. The covered stairway on the down side is visible at the back of the shelter.

There were few changes by 1954. Quite remarkably, the same three fire buckets and the porter's trolley which appeared at one end of the shelter on the up platform in 1922 are in the same place in 1954. Live rails had been added in 1925, with breaks at the staff foot-crossing in the centre of the station. The telegraph pole bears more wires, the gas lamp posts and the station name-boards have been changed and the advertise-ments removed. A platform extension appears in the foreground, with a surface of blacktop rather than wood. These were changes sufficiently slight as to leave the traveller of the 1920s, or of the 1870s, in little doubt about his location. However, when a photograph was taken from the same place in 1964, little had survived. The only links with earlier views were parts of the under-bridge and concrete coping stones from the edge of the platform extension. By coincidence, corresponding lines in North and South London, one to the Alexandra Palace and one to the Crystal Palace, closed in the same year.

FIVE

South West London and beyond

Nearly all the major railway companies were represented in central London, and in the three sectors looked at so far, no one company was completely dominant. To the north, the GN straddled a boundary with lines in both the north west and north east sectors, and in the south the LBSC was active in both south west and south east. Perhaps the most varied sector from a pre-grouping company point of view, was the north west, with the LNW, and GW and the underground lines all conspicuous. In the north east, GE dominance was slightly diminished by the presence of the LTS and underground companies. The south east was shared by the LCD and the SE, although there was a decline in distinction after the rapprochment of 1899. With the north east as 'runner-up', the south west provided the nearest approach to 'one company territory'. The LBSC and the Metropolitan District appeared on the borders, but their penetration of LSW territory was slight. Housing development between the wars affected the south west, but whereas in GW and LMS territory much of the new traffic had gone to the underground companies, in LSW (from 1923, Southern) territory, they were kept at bay. The only significant new penetration was the extension of a tube line from Clapham to Morden in 1926, on the border between the LBSC and LSW. Further penetration was checked by the electrification of existing lines and by taking over from the underground group the construction of a new line, the Wimbledon and Sutton, completed in 1930. A second new line from Motspur Park to Leatherhead was opened as far as Chessington South in 1939. Further construction was delayed by the war and then abandoned because of a green belt policy, which checked further housing development.

Since the war, major new developments have been restricted to north of the Thames, with the exception of the Victoria line tube extension to Brixton. In the south west, freight traffic has declined. Local goods depots have been closed, together with the important terminal at Nine Elms. Through traffic, from the north and midlands to the south west was routed via Feltham and that for the south and east followed the route through Kew and Clapham Junction. This has diminished. Passenger traffic, both through and local, is more dominant than ever before, but change has consisted of consolidation rather than major development. Since the war, no passenger stations have been opened and none have been closed. Of all the sectors looked at, it is in south west London and beyond that the rail passenger from the 1930s would find the least change.

Abbreviations

BR(SR)	British Railways (Southern Region)
LBSCR	London Brighton and South Coast Railway
LBSC&LSW JT.	London Brighton and South Coast and London and South Western joint
LCDR	London Chatham and Dover Railway
LPTB	London Passenger Transport Board

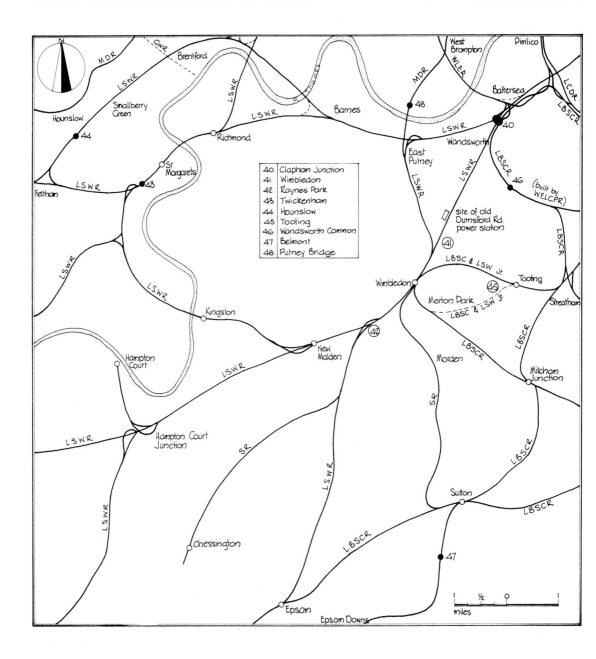

40	Clapham Junction
41	Wimbledon
42	Raynes Park
43	Twickenham
44	Hounslow
45	Tooting
46	Wandsworth Common
47	Belmont
48	Putney Bridge

LSWR	London and South Western Railway
LRT	London Regional Transport
LTB	London Transport Board
LTE	London Transport Executive
MDR	Metropolitan District Railway
SR	Southern Railway
WELCPR	West End of London and Crystal Palace Railway

Undertakings in bold lettering, in the main took over from the original companies. For the main lines there were two stages — 'take over' by the 'Big Four' in 1923, and then by British Railways in 1948. For the underground railways, there was one principal stage, take over by LPTB in 1923. (This was succeeded in turn by LTE, LTB, LTE and LRT.)

Clapham Junction 1906

40 Clapham Junction LSWR & LBSCR/SR/SR/ BR(SR) P
*c.**1906**/25 July **1981**/1 April **1986** TQ 272754*

There are both similarities and contrasts between Finsbury Park Station in north London and Clapham Junction in the south of London. Both are major points for passengers changing trains, and both were served by the trains of a number of companies (for Clapham Junction, LSWR, LBSCR and LNWR). However, two, and later three of the lines serving Finsbury Park were carried in underground tubes, whereas Clapham Junction is served exclusively by surface railways. Both stations were opened some years after the railways on which they were situated. In the case of Clapham Junction, the section of the London and Southampton Railway traversing the site was opened in 1838. A station named Wandsworth, from 1846 named Clapham Common, was opened about a quarter of a mile (½ km) west of the junction. The site first became a junction in

Clapham Junction 1981

1846 when the LSW line to Richmond, later extended to Windsor, was opened. In 1856, the West End of London and Crystal Palace Railway Company, starting from Crystal Palace, reached a secluded spot on Wandsworth Common. When in 1858 it became clear that the LSW were unwilling to agree to a junction on the site subsequently occupied by Clapham Junction Station, the WELCP was extended beyond it to a terminus on the south bank of the river, called

Pimlico. (This was replaced in 1860 by Victoria.) In 1863, the West London Extension Railway was opened from Kensington, to Battersea. In its final form, it divided into four branches, of which two led to junctions with the WELCP and the LSW Windsor lines respectively. The new Clapham Junction Station was opened with platforms on all four lines — the West London Extension (joint GW, LNW, LSW, and LBSC), the WELCP (LBSC), the LSW main line and the LSW Windsor lines. Subsequent widenings and rebuildings have produced the present station, with its 17 platforms. Buildings consisting mainly of wood and glass on the LSW side were badly damaged by

Clapham Junction 1986

fire in 1981, and at present, a major rebuilding project is in progress.

All three views were taken from the country end of the LBSC side with platforms 11/12, which formed the boundary between the LSW and the LBSC sides, in a prominent position. Platform 11 was used mainly by local trains on the LSW main line; the opposite side, nearer the camera, served the LBSC up main line. The first view, taken about 1906, shows an unidentified locomotive of the LSW 0-4-2 A12 or Jubilee class, designed by William Adams. (They were known collectively, as the Jubilee Class, because one batch had been produced by Nine Elms works in 1887, the year of Queen Victoria's Golden Jubilee.) The Jubilees were used for stopping passenger services and freight, and in particular for day excursions and troop trains. The rolling stock consisted of typical LSW bogie coaches with separate compartments. Beyond the train, the LSW buildings, located on platforms 9/10 are visible, associated with long platform canopies. The station was built at a point of transition between cutting and embankment, with communication between the 17 platforms by both bridge and subway. The west end of the station, shown in all the views, was in a cutting. The foreground of the 1906 view is occupied by empty coal wagons, being returned from the LBSC system to the West London line, and probably bound for South Wales. (The second wagon from the right belonged to the Tredegar Iron and Coal Co.) Tall signal posts of the type favoured by the LBSC, appear on the right of the photograph.

The second view was taken from a train on the LBSC up local line, after the fire of 1981. The end of platforms 13/14 appears in the foreground, with 11/12 beyond. A post with two arms in the first view, and one arm later, appears in all three views, at the end of platform 11/12. Another detail in all three views is the finial at one end of the LSW building, together with the canopy over platforms 9/10. Presumably the reason for the siting of both the lengthy canopy and the main

building over platform 9/10 was that, until the re-arrangement of the tracks in 1936, up and down LSW main line trains would have used the opposite sides of this island platform. The views of 1906 and 1981 permit comparison of the buildings before and after the fire, while that of 1986 shows rebuilding in progress. Clapham Junction owes its size to its role as a junction. The recent introduction of calls by through trains between the north and south of England, together with additional calls by trains on the LSW main line, has increased its importance. At the present time, a major re-building programme is in progress.

41 Wimbledon LSWR/SR/BR(SR)
22 April 1925/21 February 1976 TQ 256720

The section of the London and Southampton railway between Nine Elms and Woking was opened in 1838, including a station at Wimbledon. Between the cuttings at Wandsworth and Wimbledon, the line crossed the valley of the River Wandle on an embankment. At later dates, three lines came in on the south side, and one on the north. This was the line opened to East Putney in 1889, joining the main line about half a mile on the London side of Wimbledon Station. In 1905 it became the first part of the LSW to be served by electric trains, although these belonged to the District Railway. The LSW announced its own electrification scheme in 1913, and this was completed in 1916. On the up side of the main line, between the River Wandle and the junction with the East Putney line, an electric train depot and also Durnsford Road Power Station were opened. (The power station was demolished, and in 1974, a new train depot was opened on its site.) Wimbledon became the most important electric train depot on the former LSW.

Both the views, showing one of the sheds of the electric train depot, were taken from the

Wimbledon 1925

Durnsford Road overbridge, looking towards Wimbledon. That of 1925, shows the up through and up local lines, all equipped with live rails. The point rodding and lower quadrant semaphore signals were operated from Durnsford Road signal box. Alongside the depot, what looks like electric trains produced from converted LBSC steam stock with blinds drawn

Wimbledon 1976

down, awaited the inauguration of electric services, to be introduced in 1925 and 1926. However, the foreground was occupied by a train of LSW steam stock, pulling out from the depot on to the up local line. This was basically an empty stock working, but peak hour passengers were carried between Earlsfield and Waterloo. Perhaps some of them felt that haulage by one of Dugald Drummond's L12 class locomotives made a distinguished start to the day. No.428, still in LSW livery in 1925, was built at Nine Elms in 1905 and with a life lengthened by the Second World War, was not withdrawn until 1951.

The view of 1976 shows all four tracks of the main line. In the middle distance the flyover of 1936 is visible. This made possible a rearrangement of track utilisation on the London side of Wimbledon so that the down local and through on one side and the up local and through on the other became the down and up local on the left, and the up through and local on the right, as shown in the 1976 view. Also in 1936, traditional mechanical signalling has been replaced by

coloured lights. The depot was extended shortly afterwards to accommodate new trains for use on the Portsmouth electrification of 1937. After the Second World War, perhaps because of the difficulty in recruiting, a single platform for the use of staff employed at the depot, was provided on the up local line. It bore a nameboard marked 'Railway Staff Halt' but is not, of course mentioned in any public timetables. The train in the 1976 view is an up semi-fast from Alton. The leading four-coach unit was No.7823, built at York in 1963, and belonging to the Southern Region 4-VEP class, classified by BR as class 423/0. In the same position as the adapted steam stock in the 1925 view, are 4-Sub units, at that time the mainstay of the suburban services operated from Wimbledon.

42 Raynes Park Station LSWR/SR/BR(SR) GP
c.1910/1 April 1986 TQ 231691

Raynes Park is an unusual station with its up and down platforms so widely separated as to appear unrelated. Predictably, this reflects its unusual history. The section of the London and Southampton which passed through Raynes Park was opened in 1838. A branch to Epsom and Leatherhead was completed in 1859. Its double track joined the main line just west of Wimbledon Station, and ran parallel on the south side for about 1½ miles (2½ km) to a point of divergence at the future site of Raynes Park Station. The next development was the 1869 extension of the Epsom line double track, parallel to the main line, on to New Malden, where it dived under the embankment, towards Kingston. In response to housing development, a station was opened at Raynes Park in 1871. Major works in 1883 and 1884 carried the four track section on to Hampton Court Junction and incorporated what had been two separate tracks from Wimbledon, into the main line. The arrangement of up and down main on the north side and up and down

local on the south was changed to using the two inner tracks for the main line and the outer tracks for local traffic. At Raynes Park the up track of the Epsom branch was diverted to pass under the main line, which at this point was on an embankment, climbing steeply to join it on the up side. This necessitated the rebuilding of the station in approximately its present form, with up and down platforms, widely separated in plan. There are no platforms for the through tracks on the main line, but the platforms on each side serve the local tracks of the main line, and also the Epsom branch. The wide separation of the platforms not only results from the lack of any platform on the through tracks, but also from their being offset, as the up Epsom track joins the main line approximately 200 yards (183 m) on the London side of the down junction.

Both views were taken on the Epsom branch arm of the pair of platforms on the down side. Although four main line and two branch line tracks pass through the station, with no platforms on the through lines, there are only four platforms to be numbered. As this numbering

Raynes Park 1910

Raynes Park 1986

commences on the up side, the down Epsom platform is No.4. In the view of about 1910, the increasing separation of the two platform canopies reflects the divergence of the main line local and the Epsom branch tracks. This increases rapidly because of the curvature of the Epsom line, which is sufficient to require a 20 mph (32 kmph) speed limit. At the time of the first view, traffic was controlled from a signal box at the junction. Semaphore arms for the up local and main line tracks, and also the wire for the Epsom branch down starter are visible. The telegraph poles carried numerous wires, indicating heavy telegraph traffic on the main line. The gas lamps and the station nameboard are standard LSW types. The trellis fencing on one side and the hedge on the other give a somewhat rustic air, appropriate to an outer suburb of 1910. However, even more distinctive is the shrubbery at the back of the platform. The approaching train consists of standard LSW bogie coaches, with compartments, hauled by an Adams Jubilee Class locomotive.

In 1986, the shrubbery and the hedge have gone, and the trellis fencing has been replaced by palings. Trees have grown at the back of the platform, obscuring the view towards the main line. The platform canopies have been replaced, and the platforms raised and re-surfaced. The track is in the same position, but equipped with a live rail, while a concrete trough, carrying electric supply cables, has been added. (The main line was electrified in 1916 and the Epsom branch in 1925.) EMU set No.5846 of BR class 455 is approaching, forming the 18.02 from Waterloo to Dorking North. The fact that passengers would find the platform on the 'wrong' side, is explained by the history of the station.

43 Twickenham Station LSWR/SR/BR(SR) GPFLHC
c.1902/1953/3 April 1954/1954 TQ 161736

Twickenham Station, on the line to Windsor, was opened in 1848, at the same time as the line. It became the junction for Kingston in 1863. In 1869 the gap between Kingston and the main line at New Malden was closed, and it was then possible for trains to run from Waterloo to Waterloo in a continuous circuit, including calls

Twickenham Station 1902

Twickenham Station 1953

at Twickenham and Kingston. Improvements made in 1882 and 1883 included a flyover to the west of the station, carrying the up line from Kingston, and in 1899 an additional up track was added from Twickenham to St. Margaret's, the next station on the London side. Services on the Kingston 'roundabout' were electrified in 1916 and to Windsor in 1930. During the 1930s, the Southern Railway, subsidised by government finance, embarked on a programme of station rebuilding. Twickenham was on the list, partly because of the demands made on its limited accommodation when international rugby football matches took place at the nearby ground.

Twickenham Station 1954

Twickenham Station 1954

Owing to the war, the opening of the new station, on the London side of the original, was delayed until 1954.

The first photograph was taken from the down platform about 1902, with passengers preparing to board the approaching steam train. The tall chimneys belong to the station building of 1848, built in a distinctive Tudor style. The up platform became an island when the flyover was constructed in 1883, with trains from Kingston normally using the outer face. Water cranes are visible at the end of the platform. Unusually near to the station building is the corrugated iron lamp room. (As lighting was by gas, this was evidently used for the signal lamps.) A step in the face of the island platform was placed to assist staff using the foot crossing.

The 1953 photograph was taken from the road bridge with the tracks spread out in order to fit on either side of the new island platform on the other side of the bridge. There is no appreciable change in the buildings since the first photograph was taken, but the electrification of 1916 is reflected in two ways. Firstly the live rail has been added, and secondly, on the right hand of the skyline a sub-station, which originally housed three rotary converters, has been built.

Of the two pictures taken in 1954, one was taken from just outside the railway fence on the up side, shortly after the closure of the 1848 station. The water cranes have already lost their hosepipes and the footbridge is being dismantled. Although the war had been over for nearly nine years, white bands to enhance visibility during the blackout may be seen on various posts. The second photograph, taken from No.4 platform of the new station, shows the original station through the arches of the overbridge. (The platform arrangement was, from left to right, island platform 4/5 for up and down trains, island platform 2/3 for up trains and trains terminating on match days, while the side platform 1 was also provided for match days. The station of 1954 differed greatly from its predecessor of 1848.

44 Hounslow Station LSWR/SR/BR(SR)
GPFLHC
c.1906/30 March 1974 *TQ 139749*

The loop line leaving the Windsor line at Barnes and rejoining it near Feltham was opened in two stages. It reached a temporary terminus, called Hounslow, but which was situated at Smallberry

Green in 1849, and was completed in 1850. The station at Hounslow was opened at the same time as the line. In 1883 a spur line at the junction at the western end of the loop enabled trains to run on a circuit from Waterloo to Waterloo via Hounslow and Twickenham. It is perhaps no coincidence that trains of the Metropolitan District railway began serving Houslow in the same year and from that date, the LSW Hounslow Station has suffered from competition. This was intensified by the electrification of the MD line in 1905, duly countered by the electrification of the Hounslow loop in 1916. The rapid growth of the district, particularly in the 1930s, provided the 1850 station with enough traffic to ensure its survival. (In 1986, it was served by four trains an hour — two Hounslow 'roundabouts' in each direction.)

The first photograph was taken from the down platform in about 1906, when, apart from the provision of a footbridge and the extension of the platforms, the station had changed little since 1850. However, the rolling stock is unusual. Steam rail motor cars were the forerunners of the electric multiple unit trains, in that the same frame was used for carrying both passengers and motive power. The LSW built 15 rail cars, of which No.1 appears in this photograph. It was built at Nine Elms works in 1904 and withdrawn in 1916. Assembled above the frame, in addition to the boiler, were driving positions at each end, a guards compartment, and separate, open saloons for first class and third class passengers. After withdrawal, the locomotive parts were scrapped, but the passenger sections had very extended lives on the push-pull services, which more or less replaced the rail motor cars.

The second view was taken in 1974 from a footbridge at the London end of the station. At this time, the goods shed survived, although goods traffic had not been handled since 1968. Re-signalling was in progress, with the semaphore signal in the foreground about to be replaced by the colour light signal on the end of the platform. A concrete footbridge had replaced

Hounslow Station 1906

Hounslow Station 1974

the earlier metal structure, and a 4-SUB unit is leaving in the down direction. The 1850 station building remained almost unchanged — the two round objects which appear above the chimney pots are floodlights. Hounslow was typical of many Middlesex stations, built in fields, and now engulfed in housing.

45 Tooting Junction LSWR and LBSCR Jt/SR/ BR(SR) GP

c.1912/13 September 1975 *TQ 278706*

In 1868, a number of lines were opened to the

Tooting Junction 1912

Tooting Junction 1975

south west of London. One of them ran across country from a junction with the LBSC near Streatham to join the LSW main line at Wimbledon. From Tooting a branch connected this with the Wimbledon and Croydon line at Merton Park. As one of the functions of the Tooting, Merton and Wimbledon Railway was to connect the LSW and LBSC systems, predictably it was operated by the two companies jointly. The station at Tooting was opened in 1868, just west of the junction of the lines to Wimbledon and to Merton, with platforms on both lines. This arrangement ended in 1894 when a new station was opened east of the junction, with the platforms reached from a station building, alongside a road bridge, which spanned the railway tracks. It was a victim of wartime closures in 1917, and was not re-opened until 1923. Electric services were introduced in 1929 over the 'main line' from Streatham to Wimbledon, but the Tooting end of the 'branch' was closed completely, and the remainder served only by steam-hauled goods trains. Tooting was no longer a junction, and in 1938, it was re-named Tooting.

The two photographs were taken from a footbridge to the west of the station. The first, taken about 1912, shows the remains of the station of 1868. The centre platform and canopy are well preserved, while the building on the up side is being used as a dwelling. The signal box, the junction, and the associated lower quadrant

signals, apparently LSW in style, are also visible. In 1975, the same view included a number of changes. The up side building is still in use as a dwelling, although all the platforms have been removed. The junction, the signal box and the signals have gone. At this time, the basic train service was from Holborn Viaduct via Herne Hill to Wimbledon and Sutton, augmented by some trains from London Bridge. The 4-EPB set 5028, allocated to Slade Green, appears in the photograph. These sets were introduced in 1951, built at Eastleigh, and were classified by BR as 415/1. Although there are other cases of the survival of parts of abandoned stations, Tooting provides an outstanding example.

46 Wandsworth Common LBSCR/SR/BR(SR)
1924/18 April 1986 TQ 277736

The West End of London and Crystal Palace Railway was opened to a temporary terminus on Wandsworth Common in 1856, pending the completion of arrangements to run over the LSW into Waterloo. When these broke down, subsequent extensions were to Pimlico in 1858 and on to Victoria in 1860. The station on the Common was replaced in 1858 by New Wandsworth Station, located just short of the point from which the lines to Victoria and Waterloo ran side by side. This was about a quarter of a mile (½ km) from Clapham Junction. In 1869, six years after the opening of Clapham Junction, a third Wandsworth station, almost on the site of the first, was opened. It was extensively rebuilt in 1895 when the line, which from 1862 had formed part of the main line from Victoria to Brighton, was quadrupled.

The two photgraphs were taken from the Common, beyond the London end of the station. The bridge carrying Bellevue Road appears in both photographs, and the four tracks are in the same position. Wandsworth Common signal box, which lasted from the quadrupling of 1895 until the provision of coloured light signals in 1952, appears in the first view. The line had been electrified on the LBSC overhead electric system in 1911. A gantry and also wooden troughing carrying cables appear in the 1924 view. The overhead system was finally displaced by third rail electrification in 1929. However, the first photograph is dominated by an up Brighton

Wandsworth Common 1924

Wandsworth Common 1986

express train. The combination of a tank locomotive and compartment coaches would be unlikely for express trains on other lines, but they were considered quite suitable for the 51 mile (82 km) run to Brighton. (In fact, the LBSC had no corridor coaches; the alternative to compartment stock was Pullman cars.) The tank locomotives were usually turned at the terminals as speed limits of 60 mph (97 kmph) running chimney first and 45 mph (72 kmph) running bunker first, were imposed. The LBSC 4-6-2T No.325 of the J1 class was built at Brighton works in 1910 to the design of D.E. Marsh. Only two

locomotives of this class were built, and until supplanted by electric trains at the end of 1932, they were used mainly between London and Brighton. No.325 had been repainted in March 1924, in the Southern Railway's green livery, and re-numbered No.B325. Later it was numbered 2325 by the Southern and 32325 by BR. Having been moved from Brighton to the Eastbourne shed, further electrification necessitated a move to Tunbridge Wells, from which 32325 was withdrawn in 1951.

In the second photograph concrete sleepers appeared on some of the tracks, and the live rail on all. The wooden troughing had disappeared, and a new sub-station had been constructed on the up side. The up train lacked a head code but as 4-CIG set No.7316 was allocated to Brighton, it may well have been an up Brighton express. These sets were introduced in 1964, were built at York and now belong to BR class 421/1. The end of the station platform is visible under the bridge. However, in this pair of photographs, the most remarkable change is in the trains.

47 Belmont Station LBSCR/SR/BR(SR) GP
c.1908/6 August 1963/1 April 1986 TQ 256621

The branch line from Sutton to Epsom Downs had something in common with the LCD branch to the Crystal Palace. They were both opened in 1865, and both served a major attraction for day excursionists — in the case of Epsom Downs, for

Belmont Station 1908

Belmont Station 1963

those going to the race track. Because of this, the terminals were far larger than local traffic would have justified. On the busiest days, such as Derby Day, all Epsom Downs' eight platforms would be in use, and three additional signal boxes would be open on the four miles of the branch to handle traffic, which would often include a Royal train. There was competition for the racecourse traffic from 1901 when SEC services were inaugurated to the rival Tattenham Corner Station, comparable, although chronologically different, to the competition between the two Crystal Palace stations. Two intermediate stations were opened on the branch, California (renamed Belmont in 1875) and Banstead. Both attracted some season ticket traffic, and also benefited from the construction of a number of large hospitals, whose long-stay patients received weekend visitors. With the mechanisation of road transport, the race traffic diminished but there were enough local passengers to justify the electrification of the branch in 1928. Season ticket traffic increased until the 1950s and then declined. One contributive factor was the increasing tendency of passengers to drive to

nearby stations, such as Epsom and Sutton, which offered a better train service. In 1982, with the reduction of peak traffic on race days, the branch had the unusual distinction among lines on the Southern electric network, of being singled. The contrast with the closure of the Crystal Palace branch reflects, in particular, rather less competition from other railway stations.

The first picture of Belmont shows the gable end of the original station building of 1865. When the station was opened, there was a level crossing at the Epsom Downs End, so that either side of the line was almost equally accessible. The reason for constructing the building on the down side, when most passengers would be departing in the up direction, might well be its proximity to a main road to Brighton. The level crossing was replaced by a bridge, and as no footbridge was provided on the platforms, this would have been used by passengers joining up trains. The accommodation on the up side consisted of a canopy and a somewhat austere waiting room. Milk churns on the up platform could have been returning empties, or have contained milk from local farms, awaiting conveyance to London. The large hospital, concealed by the trees, might have received milk by rail. The tall building in front of

Belmont Station 1986

the trees provided hospital staff accommodation. The signal box, which in addition to normal train control, had been responsible for level crossing operation and also access to the goods yard, was south of the bridge from which this photograph was taken, but the up starter semaphore signal is visible. In 1906 the LBSC ordered 15 trailer cars for use on push-pull trains, and one of these is approaching the station from the Sutton direction. Although not visible, the locomotive was probably a tank engine of either the D or of the Terrier class.

The second photograph was taken in 1963. The station building was destroyed in the war, but in 1963 the temporary premises are still in use. The features on the up side, including the railway structures, are virtually unchanged, although in this photograph the main hospital buildings are visible to the right of the staff quarters. Train services had been electrified since 1928, and a 4-SUB set is leaving for London. Although an electric train, it carried an oil tail lamp. The final view shows Belmont after the line was singled. As the peak hour service consisted of two trains per hour, and trains took ten minutes to traverse the branch, the single track was proving sufficient. At Belmont, new buildings were constructed on the former down side and the up side platform was abandoned. Outside the railway building, the Victorian hospital staff building has been demolished. The train is the 11.22 from Victoria, consisting of class 455 set No.5815. The line and the station survives but is much changed from the days when King Edward VII would have passed through on his way to Epsom Downs.

48 Putney Bridge Station MDR/LPTB/LTE/LTB/LRT P*

c.1900/3 June 1986 TQ 245759

The LSW extended into Middlesex and the Metropolitan District penetrated Surrey. The MD reached Wimbledon in stages, as far as West Brompton in 1869, and on to Putney Bridge in 1880. The District line terminated there until 1889, when the LSW opened a railway from an end on junction with the MD to join the main line at Wimbledon. The stations on the LSW line were served by the trains of both companies until 1941, when the LSW withdrew their service. The MD service was electrified in 1905 and the LSW in 1915. A proportion of the District line trains always terminated at Putney Bridge, and in 1910 the tracks were re-arranged to facilitate their reversal. Since then, changes have been matters of detail.

Both photographs were taken at the London end of the up (or eastbound) platform. The first, taken before electrification, shows No.44, a 4-4-0 tank locomotive, constructed by Beyer Peacock for the MD in 1884. It carried a destination board marked 'Putney Bridge'. Spending most of its time underground, it had no cab, and could consume its own steam. The pipes for carrying steam from the cylinders to the water tanks are visible, and also the pipe, with central inlet, for feeding water to the side tanks. The train consisted of four-wheel compartment stock with gas lighting. As far as Walham Green, (now Fulham Broadway), the MD ran below ground, but across the low lying land towards the river it was carried on a viaduct. This was one of the reasons why the platforms were made of wood. Because Putney Bridge was used as a terminus, starting signals for the up or eastbound direction were provided for both tracks, that on the left apparently fixed to the corner of the signal box. Below the main signals, smaller arms were provided to control access to the locomotive siding. (The first coach is crossing the connection to it, and its position is indicated by the top of the water tank, seen above the coaches.) This was the period noted for enamel advertisements and a number of examples can be seen.

The 1905 electrification of the MD employed a live rail and a separate rail for returning current. The re-arrangement of tracks in 1910 included

Putney Bridge 1900

Putney Bridge 1986

the provision of an island platform and a separate track for trains terminating at Putney Bridge. The view of 1986 shows both features. Coloured light signals have replaced semaphores. (The signal for the up or eastbound through platform is obscured by the mirror, provided for the motormen of trains operating without guards, in order to check the closing of the sliding doors.) The substitution of electric traction for steam is reflected in the disappearance of the engine siding and the electric cables spanning the tracks.

The platform surface consists of blacktop and concrete slabs with a whitewashed edge. The contrast in the trains is at least as great as that in the tracks and the station. Electricity has replaced steam for traction and gas for lighting; sliding doors and open coaches are provided instead of compartments and slam doors. The leading car, No.7126, was delivered to LT in 1983, and with its unpainted aluminium bodywork is very representative of change in London Transport.

SELECT BIBLIOGRAPHY

Barker, T.C. and Robbins, Michael *A history of London transport*, Vol. I, Allen and Unwin, 1963; Vol. II, Allen and Unwin, 1974.

Borley, H.V. *Chronology of London railways* Railway and Canal Historical Society 1982.

Course, Edwin *London railways* Batsford, 1962.

Course, Edwin *Bexleyheath railway* Oakwood, 1981.

Davies, R. & Grant, M.D. *London and its railways* David and Charles, 1982

Howard Turner, J.T. *The London, Brighton and South Coast Railway*, Vol. I, Batsford, 1977; Vol. II, Batsford, 1978; Vol. III, Batsford, 1979.

Jackson, Alan A. *London's local railways* David and Charles, 1978.

Jackson, Alan A. *London's termini* David and Charles, 2nd Edn., 1985.

Jackson, Alan A. *London's Metropolitan Railways* David and Charles, 1986.

White, H.P. *A regional history of the railways of Great Britain*. Vol. III: *Greater London* David and Charles, 1963.

Wrottesley, John *The Great Northern Railway*, Vol. I, Batsford, 1979; Vol. II, Batsford, 1979; Vol. III, Batsford, 1981.